Bramha Vidya

First Published by

ISBN: 978-93-5819-136-3

Price: INR 160

BLUEROSE PUBLISHERS
www.bluerosepublishers.com
info@bluerosepublishers.com
+91 8882 898 898

Dedicated to

Acharyas and Lord LakshmiNrisimha

FOREWORD

By VKR Mantracalam Swamy

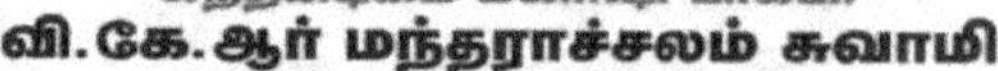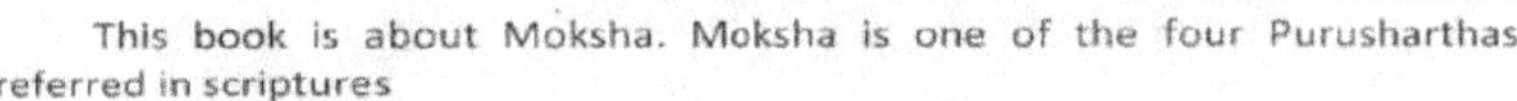

This book is about Moksha. Moksha is one of the four Purusharthas referred in scriptures (Literatures). Once some one attains Moksha (there are various explanations and methods suggested by our Gurus, and the important one is to get Brahma Vidya (Knowledge about absolute truth from a practitioner Guru). Moksha releases one from miseries and gives a stop to birth and death cycle. This is attainable by any one irrespective of caste, gender or race by sincerely following certain path as given by our Gurus.

The other three are Dharma, Artha and Kama. Dharma is the path of righteousness, artha is prosperity with wealth and Kama is desire to execute any activity and pleasure. Out of all these Moksha is considered as the Supreme and human birth is essentially to attain the Moksha.

In this book, my student, and Atma, Adhi Mitran Sri. K. V. Krishnan, shows a path as per his learning from the lineage of Ahobilamutt, NyAsA, complete surrender to Supreme God, the Creator.

He has explained in detail from VedA, Upanishads and other Scriptures some views to learn the Knowledge (Vidya) about Brahmam from a Guru and quoted many scriptures in support of his scholarly work.

He stated about Para and Apara Vidya also and chose Apara Vidya, to be pursued in comparison to Para Vidya. Brahma Vidya is dealt in both Vidyas and there are 32 Vidyas according to his quotes which if one follows attaining Moksha is easy. But he recommends total surrender (Nysa Vidya) as the simplest and easy route to MokshA.

He also quotes from his Gurus about Lord NarAyaNA and He being the Brahmam.

I pray Sri. Lakshmi NrasimhA, and His Lotus feet to shower His grace on Sri. Krishnan, my Astrology student all the best in his endeavour.

Maha Guru Mantracalam

By TK Parthasarathy, Professor, Madras University

BRAHMA VIDYA by Dr. K V KRISHNAN is a wonderful attempt to showcase what is the foundation for SANÂTANA DHARMA to all Indians, particularly to the younger generation, who are yet to be exposed to our culture and tradition and the author deserves all appreciation.

Dr. K V KRISHNAN has studied deeply our traditions and possesses a deep knowledge, but the most appreciable thing in him is that he wants to share his knowledge with others through this book. He has a plethora of qualifications and has obtained a doctorate in Vedic Astrology. He is a versatile scholar in the Upaniṣads too.

Brahmavidya is the branch of scriptural knowledge derived primarily through a study of *Prasthâna Trayi* the Upanishads, Brahma Sutras, and the Bhagavad Gita. Starting from four *Puruṣârthas* - Dharma, Artha, Kâma, and Mokṣa which have an equivalent four stages in Tamil too-

அறம்,பொருள்,இன்பம் வீடு, our country is the most spiritualistic country and our Hinduism believes in it very strongly. Even other Indigenous religions like Buddhism, Jainism, and Sikhism –all believe in the spiritual experiences of the individual. We believe in *Pâpam and Puṇyam* which are unique to our thinking and have no parallel in the West. For the West, the *âtma* –the human soul is only a sinner and has to be redeemed. For us, the *âtma* is *sat, cit, and ânantha-* true, knowledgeable, and blissful. The *âtma* if allowed to travel in the righteous path in this tinsel world, it is sure to attain the *parama puruṣârtham-* the *mokṣa.*

As Nammâzhâr says "வைகுந்தம் புகுவது மண்ணவர் விதியே" –all human beings on earth have the right to enter the Lord's domain (*Śrī Vaikuṇṭa*) as none is a sinner. This we learn from the Brahma Vidhya through Upanisads and the author has profusely quoted from various esoteric scriptures to stress on this point.

The author has left no subject under Sanatana untouched and his write-up on Yoga is currently becoming a universal feature In the words of the author, "To escape from the cycle of births and deaths is possible only through Yogic discipline, complete faith, affection, in Brahman and feeling His presence in countless manifestations" is noteworthy.

Dr. K V KRISHNAN is an example of a true Viṣṇavite as whenever I tried to reach him over the phone, he is into anuṣṭanam a rarity in the contemporary world. It is very easy to possess knowledge if you have a true Acharyan, but developing anuṣṭanam as your way of life is well neigh impossible in the contemporary world with so many attractions and temptations. *gnânam* and *anuṣṭanam* are like two feathers of a bird and sans one he is not a full-vaiṣṇavite, our forefathers have recorded. He is endowed with both these.

I wish him all the best and script many such books like this which will throw light on our age-old sampradâya which will guide our posterity in the path that is to be adhered to.

T K PARTHASARATHY

By Jyothishakalanidhi Dr. S. Suyamprakash MA. Ph.

Sree Guruvayurappan Jyothisha Vigyana Kalaakendram

"Jyothishakalanidhi" **Dr. S. Suyamprakash**, MA. Ph.D.

Sree Guruvayurappan Jyothisha Vigyana Kalaakendram, 101, Chennimalai Road, Erode -638 002.

(0424) 2275717, 2275818   suyampragash@gmail.com, kalaakendram@gmail.com

10ᵗʰ May 2023,
Erode

Hindu scriptures refer to four purusharthas (objects of human pursuit) ; namely dharma (righteousness), artha (prosperity), kama (pleasure) and moksha (liberation or the spiritual freedom). All the four purusharthas are said to be important, but moksha is considered to be the supreme ideal of life.

Moksha is the spiritual freedom as the eternal and indestructible status which is free from all misery. Such a state of being can be attained by anyone - irrespective of his or her race, gender or caste etc. - by sincerely pursuing the spiritual path.

Brahmavidya (derived from the Sanskrit words brahma and vidyā) is that branch of scriptural knowledge derived primarily through a study of the veda mantras & upanishads. Put together, it means knowledge of the mantra/absolute. Brahmavidya is considered to be the highest ideal of classical Hinduism.

In the Puranas, this is divided into two branches, the first one dealing with the vedic mantras and is called para vidya or former knowledge, and the latter dealing with the study of the upanishads and is called the apara vidya or latter knowledge.

Both para and apara vidya constitute brahma vidya. There is a separate upanishad on Brahma vidya called Brahma vidyopanishad. Brahma Vidya Upanishad is the 40th among the 108 Upanishads. It contains 110 verses and found attached in Krishna Yajur Veda. Brahma Vidya is the knowledge of Brahman. Hence this Upanishad deals with the knowledge of Brahman.

Vedas declare,
nārāyaṇaḥ paraṁ brahma tattvaṁ nārāyaṇaḥ paraḥ,
nārāyaṇaḥ paro jyotirātmā nārāyaṇaḥ paraḥ.
nārāyaṇaḥ paro dhyātā dhyānam nārāyaṇaḥ paraḥ.

The Lord Narayana is the Supreme Absolute; Narayana is the Supreme Reality; Narayana is the Supreme Light; Narayana is the Supreme Self; Narayana is the Supreme Meditator; Narayana is the Supreme Meditation.

This book is a humble attempt to identify the secret of Brahma Vidya, in the name Vishnu who commands over the marvelous deeds.

Praying to the lotus feet of Srimannarayana to shower his grace on us.

Jyothishakalanidhi **Dr. S. Suyamprakash**, MA. Ph.D.
Sree Guruvayurappan Jyothisha Vigyana Kalaakendram
Erode

By BVK Sastry - Yoga-Samskrutham University

It serves as a good resource book for a one day
workshop with Vak-yoga practical; and parts
of Vak-yoga courses. Good Work.

By Tina - IQViA

I read the topic - How do we liberate ourselves
- you have written it very nicely and clearly.

Acknowledgements

My sincere thanks to ..

My wife Sow. K. Rama

for her moral support and selfless help throughout this effort
without which I could not have completed this book

My nephew VK Ranga in Atlanta, GA

for immense help towards desktop editing and publishing

My long time associate Ms. Hemalatha

for her help in forming a mobile app to convert Devanagari script to IAST

My daughter Sow. K.Hemamalini

for her ardent support in completing this work

My Son Chi. Madhusudan's colleague from IQViA, Mumbai, Ms. Tina

for her encouraging manuscript review

Contents

1. Prayer

ज्ञानानन्दमयं देवं निर्मल स्फकाकृतिम्।
आधारं सर्व विद्यानां **हयग्रीवम्** उपास्महे।।

अज्ञानतिमिरान्धस्य ज्ञानाञ्जनशलाकया।
चक्षुरुन्मीलितं येन तस्मै श्रीगुरवे नमः।।

गुरुर्ब्रह्मा गुरुर्विष्णुःगुरुर् देवोमहेश्वरः।
गुरुर् साक्षात् परब्रह्म तस्मै **श्रीगुरवे** नमः।।

यो नित्यम् अच्युतपदाम्बुजयुग्मरुक्म-
व्यामोहतस्तदितराणि तृणाय मेने ।

अस्मद् गुरोर्भगवतोऽस्य दयैकसिन्धोः
रामानुजस्य चरणौ शरणं प्रपद्ये ॥

श्रीमान् वेङ्कटनाथार्यः कवितार्किककेसरी ।
वेदान्ताचार्यवर्यो मे सन्निधत्तां सदा हृदि ॥

2. Introduction

Brahma Vidya - the knowledge of Truth, that results in Self-realization followed by realisation of Brahmam within us, whereby one remains untouched by any situation in life. Brahmam is the neuter gender of the root word-form "brih" that means big. As the word big has not been further qualified to reveal its dimension, we must understand that Brahmam, the word means that which is free from all forms of limitation.

ब्रह्म and Vidya. ब्रह्म comes from root word ब्ह् means biggest and nothing equal or superior to the same. विद्या, comes from विद्- to know. As the word big has not been further qualified to reveal its dimension, we must understand that Brahmam, the word means that which is free from all forms of limitation. Different methods of approaching the Absolute or real truth, the Brahmam, are known as Vidyas or UpAsanAs.

Following pages discusses these various Vidyas (thirty two as stated in VedA) by means of which the Jiva or the individual soul attains **Brahman or the Supreme Soul (Liberation from Cycle of Birth and death)**. The focus in this article will discuss philosophy as enumerated by Sri. Bhagavat RamAnujar (VishishtAdvaita philosophy). Other major philosophy enumerated by Adi Sankara, the Advaitam concept is also discussed, with the help of Internet sources and Books published by various scholars, Kalakshepams from Specialist Vidwans as given in Bibliography.

The secret of Brahmavidyā is to reveal the real nature of the Ātmā, that is all-pervading, that is like ghee in the milk, that is the source of **<u>Atmavidyā</u>** and **<u>Tapas</u>** and to show that everything is in essence one. This is the English translation of the Brahma Upanishad (belonging to the Krishna-Yajurveda).

3. Brahmam as stated In Purusha Suktam

वेदाहमेतं पुरुषं महान्तमादित्यवर्णं तमसःपरस्तात् ।

तमेवविदित्वाति मृत्युमेति नान्यपन्थाविद्यतेयनाय ॥(श्वेताश्वतरोपनिषद्-8)

vēdāhamētaṁ puruṣaṁ mahāntamādityavarṇaṁ tamasaḥparastāt |

tamēvaviditvādi   mr̥tyumēti   nānyaḥ   panthā   vidyatēyanāya||

(Swetasvataropanishad-8)

Meaning of the above mantra:

God is the supreme reality who shines effulgent like the Sun beyond all darkness and exists everywhere. We should know His numerous attributes, and try to experience His presence within us and outside. One passes beyond death only on realizing Him (God-the supreme reality). There is no other way of escape from the cycle of births and deaths.

Escape from the cycle of births and deaths is possible only through **Yogic** discipline, complete faith, affection, in Brahmam and feeling His presence in countless manifestations. (As Lord Krishna advises in Gita- to understand His Avatara Rahasya). A very good **Subhashitani**, about Vidya is given below. Virtually Vidya could give everything including appreciation and pooja by kings. Even if wealth is not with someone if Vidya is there, that is sufficient and those who do not have vidya are equal to पशुः i.e., animal. Vidya is equated to Supreme devata, which is what is **Brahma Vidya.**

विद्या नाम नरस्य रूपमधिकं प्रच्छन्नगुप्तं धनम्

विद्या भोगकरी यशः सुखकरी विद्या गुरूणां गुरुः |

विद्या बन्धुजनो विधेषगमने **विद्या परा देवता**

विद्या राजसु पूज्यते न तु धनं विद्याविहीनः पशुः॥

vidyā nāma narasya rūpamadhikaṁ pracchatraguptaṁ dhanam

vidyā bhōgakarī yaśaḥ bukhārī vidyā gurūṇāṁ guruḥ |

vidyā bandhujanō vidhēṣagamanē vidyā parā dēvatā

vidyā rājasu pūjyatē na tu dhanaṁ vidyāvihīnaḥ paśuḥ||

Another Subhashitani for VidyA:

नास्ति विद्या समं सक्षु नास्ति विद्या समं तपः |

नास्ति राग समं दुःखम् नास्ति त्याग समं सुखम् ||

nāsti vidyā samaṁ sakṣu nāsti vidyā samaṁ tapaḥ |

nāsti rāga samaṁ duḥkham nāsti tyāga samaṁ sukham ||

There is no such sight such as knowledge. **(विद्या)** i.e., **by knowledge one can see what cannot be seen by naked eye. Knowledge gives the vision to see beyond some obvious things. That is how by learning Brahma VidyA through a Guru one can see Brahmam. (Maitreyi-VidyA-Refer page no 15/40-Sr No 27)**

There is no Tapha (Hard work let us say) such as Truth. One has to do lot of hard work to be on the side of Truth.

There is no Sorrow such as the desire. There is no happiness such as sacrifice. Who else would be happier and more satisfied, than our own Mother? (nAsti tyAga samam sukham)

4. Contents of the Brahma Upaniṣad

The temple of human body

In the heart are all gods,

In it the vital breaths also,

In the heart is life and light,

And the threefold thread of the world.

Prana soars to heights when awake and retires during deep sleep, states the text, just like the falcon soars to the skies and returns to its nest in the night.

Śaunaka Mahāśala questioned the holy Sage <u>Pippalāda</u> thus: "In this beautiful <u>Brahmapura</u> of body, the fit residence of divine beings, how are (the deities of) Vak, etc., located? How do they function? To whom belongs this power? He to whom this power belongs, what is He?"

Pippalāda then having deeply considered, imparted to him the <u>Brahmavidyā</u> (divine wisdom), that most excellent of all things. "It is <u>Prāṇa</u> (i.e.,) Ātmā. It is Ātmā that exercises this power. It is the life of all <u>Devas.</u> It is their death and (their) life. Brahman that shines pure, resplendent, and all-pervading, in this divine Brahmapura (of body), rules (all). The Jīva (identifying himself with) the Indriyas, rules them like a spider. The spider throws out from a single thread out of his body a whole web, and draws it into himself by that same thread; so Prāṇa, whenever it goes, draws after it the objects of its creation (Vāk, etc.). During Suṣupti, (the Prāṇa) goes to its seat (Brahman) through the Nādis . Just as a child obtains happiness without desiring for it (in play), so also Devadatta obtains happiness in Suṣupti. He certainly knows, (being) Param-Jyotis, and the person desiring Jyotis, enjoys bliss in the contemplation of Jyotis. Then he comes back to the dream-plane by the same way, like a caterpillar. It remaining on a blade of grass, first puts forward its foot on another blade in front, conveys its body to it, and having got a firm hold of it, then only leaves the former and not before. So, this is the Jāgrata state. As this (Devadatta) bears at the same time eight skulls, so this Jāgrata, the source of Devas and Vedas, clings to a man like the breasts in a woman. During the Jāgrata avasthā, merit and demerit are postulated of this Deva(power); he is capable of great expansion and is the inner mover. He is Khaga, (bird), Karkata (crab), Puṣkara (ākāś), prāṇa, pain, parāpara, Ātmā and Brahman. This deity causes to know.

He who knows thus obtains Brahman, the supreme, the support of all things, and the Kṣetrajña. He obtains Brahman, the supreme, support of all things, and the Kṣetrajña. "The Pursuha has four seats—navel, heart, neck, and head. There Brahman with the four feet specially shines. Those feet are jāgrata, svapna, suṣupti, and turya. In jāgrata he is Brahmā, in svapna Vishnu, in suṣupti Rudra, and in turya the supreme Akṣara. He is Aditya, Viṣṇu, Īśvara, Puruṣa, prāṇa, jīva, agni, the resplendent. The Para-Brahman shines in the midst of these. He is without manas, ear, hands, feet, and light. There the worlds are no worlds, Devas no Devas, Vedas no Vedas, sacrifices no sacrifices, mother no mother, father no father, daughter-in-law no daughter-in-law, hermits no hermits; so, one only Brahman shines as different. In the Hṛdayākāś (ākāś in the heart) is the Cidākāś. That is Brahman. It is extremely subtle. The Hṛdayākāś can be known. This moves in it. In Brahman, everything is strung. Those who thus know the Lord know everything.

In him the Devas, the worlds, the Pitṛs and the Ṛṣis do not rule. He who has awakened knows everything. All the Devas are in the heart; in the heart are all the prāṇas: in the heart are prāṇa, jyotis and that three-plied holy thread. In the heart in Caitanya,

it (prāṇa) is. Put on the yajñopavīta (holy thread), the supreme, the holy, which came into existence along with the Prajāpati, which gives long life and which is very excellent; let this give you strength and tejas. Those whose tuft of hair is jñāna, who are firmly grounded in jñāna, consider jñāna only as supreme. Jñāna is holy and excellent. He whose śikhā (tuft of hair) is jñāna like the śikhi (flame of agni)—he, the wise one, only wears a true śikhā; others wear a mere tuft of hair. Those brāhmaṇas and others who perform the ceremonies prescribed in the Vedas—they wear this thread only as a symbol of their ceremonies. Those who know the Vedas say that he only is a true brāhmaṇa who wears the śikhā of jñāna and whose yajñopavīta is the same (jñāna). This yajñopavīta (Yajña means Viṣṇu or sacrifice and Upavīta is that which surrounds; hence that which surrounds Viṣṇu) is supreme and is the supreme refuge. He who wears that really knows—he only wears the sūtra, he is Yajña (Viṣṇu) and he only knows Yajña (Viṣṇu).

One God hidden in all things, pervades all things and is the Inner Life of all things. He awards the fruits of <u>karma</u>, he lives in all things, he sees all things without any extraneous help, he is the soul of all, there is nothing like him, He is the great wise one. He is the one doer among the many action-less objects. He is always making one thing appear as several (by <u>SankalpA</u>). Those wise men who see him in <u>buddhi</u>, they only obtain eternal peace.

Having made Ātmā as the (upper) <u>araṇi</u> (attritional piece of wood) and <u>Praṇava</u> the lower araṇi, by constant practice of dhyāna one should see the concealed deity. As the oil in the sesamum seed, as the <u>ghee</u> in the curds, as the water in the rivers, and as the fire in the araṇi, so they who practise truth and austerities see Him in the buddhi.

As the spider throws out and draws into itself the threads, so the jīva goes and returns during the jāgrata and the svapna states. The heart is in the form of a closed lotus-flower, with its head hanging down; it has a hole in the top. Know it to be the great abode of All.

Know that during jāgrata it (jīva) dwells in the eye, and during svapna in the throat; during suṣupti, it is in the heart and during turya in the head. (Because buddhi unites) the Pratyag-ātma with the Paramātma, the worship of <u>sandhyā</u> (union) arose. So, we should perform sandhyāvandana (rites).

The sandhyāvandana performed by dhyāna requires no water. It gives no trouble to the body or the speech. That which unites all things is the sandhyā of the one-staffed (sannyāsins). Knowing That from which speech and mind turn back without being able to obtain it and That which is the bliss of Jīva, the wise one is freed.

From Brahma Vidya Upanishad: (Swamini Vimalananda's notes)

Desire is the root cause of all knowledge, action and thinking. We believe that success is to achieve all we desire. Yet most of us do not succeed in fulfilling most of our desires, despite sincere efforts.

The eighth chapter of the Chandogya <u>Upanishad</u> drives home the fact that a state of total fulfilment of desires (Satya kama) is attained through **Brahma Vidya - the knowledge of Truth,** that results in Self-realization followed by realisation of Brahmam within us, whereby one remains untouched by any situation in life.

Indra, the king of heaven lived for 101 years in the hermitage of Prajapati, the Creator, in order to gain this knowledge and experience. A life of Self-control and meditation on the heart-space was the means taught, and total freedom and fulfilment, (the goal) was achieved. Desire is the root of all knowledge, action and thinking. It is the cause of our entire Samsara with all its grief, stress and strain.

Yet all of us seek only to fulfil our desires. We believe that freedom is to be able to do what we want, i.e., fulfil all our desires. Success is to achieve all we desire and happiness is to enjoy all we desired. Rather than seeking a state of desire-lessness, we wish to attain a state wherein we can fulfil all that we desire. And therefore, we are envious of people who have everything they desire? We feel attracted to and worship those who can produce and attain anything by mere will or wish? We daydream of indulging and gorging on all we desire? Would it not be wonderful if all we wanted came to us without us having to lift our little finger?

Such a state of fulfilment of desires (Satya KAma, Satya Sankalpa) is promised to us by the Scriptures and the wise through Self-realization. The Self is infinite and infinity alone is Bliss (Bhumaiva sukham). All objects and pleasures are included in the infinite Self and therefore Self-realization is a state of fulfilment of all desires. (According to Sri. RamAnujA this is step-1, and further one has to realise the absolute truth or reality, the Brahman, ultimate through one of the Brahma Vidyas) However, mere intellectual knowing does not result in Self-realization.

Being already one with us, Self-realization is not possible through any or many worldly actions or spiritual practices. Then how do we attain it?

One must meditate on it to realize it. Is meditation difficult? Can one meditate without a religious background? Is there any universal symbol of the Self/Truth that all can identify with? How long does it take? Is the practice interesting or tedious? 'I' am the centre of my life and of supreme interest to myself. Others may be indifferent to me, but my entire world revolves around me and 'I' alone am the focus of all my thoughts and efforts. Hence, meditation on the Self would seem quite natural and effortless. But that is not so. The pure Self, nameless and formless, (the AtmA) is extremely subtle and therefore a symbol or support is required to help our extroverted mind to refocus. The heart-space within, which is always available as 'here and now', is a universal symbol of the Self. Anyone irrespective of their religion, nationality, caste, creed or cline can meditate on it. Such meditation leads to Self- realization and a state of fulfilment of all desires. (This is one such Brahma Vidya- advised by Upanishad.)

However, such meditation is possible only for one, who is self-controlled, is capable of managing one's mind and senses, and is able to sublimate one's Vasanas-impressions of pleasure and pain practiced and etched in our psyche over lifetimes. Control over even the most basic instincts like sex and other such compulsive and instinctive impressions render the mind subtle, pure, and focused, so that one can meditate on the Self. **Strange, but true indeed, that the control of desires is the means recommended to ultimately attain a state of total fulfilment of desires! This is the very theme of the eighth chapter of the Chandogya Upanishad.**

The Chandogya Upanisad forms part of the Brahmana-s of the Talavakara section of the Sama Veda. Like all Upanisad-s, its main topic is the Knowledge of the Truth (Brahma Vidya). However, the first five chapters mainly describe a variety of rituals (karma-s) and methods of worship and meditation (Upasana) catering to different types of people. The last three chapters predominantly propound Self-knowledge.

This Upanisad introduces us to endearing and earnest seekers of Truth like Narada, Satyakama and Svetaketu and compassionate teachers like Aruni, Sanatkumara and Prajapati. The stories and dialogues between different Guru-s and disciples teach us many important lessons of life.

In chapter VIII, one learns from Indra, sincerity and the patience required to gain great goals.

In the sixth chapter, through the story of Sage Uddalaka and his disciple-son, Shvetaketu, it was shown that the Truth alone really exists. Existence alone is the Truth and that Existence alone is the True Nature. All the names and forms experienced are only modifications superimposed on the Truth. The Truth is subtle and difficult to comprehend.

In the seventh chapter the Truth is indicated through the various superimposed modifications progressing gradually from the gross to the subtle. Finally, one realizes the Truth, which is beyond the gross and the subtle and designated here as Brahman-the Infinite. This chapter also takes us through a range of meditations from the gross to the subtle thereby making us fit for meditation on the highest Truth.

In the final chapter of the Chandogya Upanishad, Prajapati, the Creator, promises agelessness, fearlessness, immortality, total freedom, and fulfilment of all desires through Self-realization. The Self is available 'here and now' to one and all and it is to be meditated upon in the 'heart-space' within.

Self-knowledge

The all pervading Atman,
Like butter concealed in milk,
In self-knowledge, self-discipline rooted,
Is the final goal of the Upanishad.

We find herein the story of Indra, the king of heaven attaining realization after living for 101 long years, a life of self-control spent in study, reflection, and meditation; and Virochana, the king of demons, living for 32 years, misunderstanding the knowledge, and spreading a materialistic and selfish doctrine.

This clearly shows the importance of a pure and subtle mind and the means to achieve it for Self-realization.

5. Prajapati Vakyam

Brahma Vidya in Bagavat Gita as stated by Sri. Alawandar (One of Sri. RamAnujA's Guru) and Sri. RamaNujA. (Prajapati Vakyam from Gitartha Sangragam and Kalakshepam of Vaikuntavasi Sri. Mannarkudi Rajagopalan, AstAna Vidvan of Sri Ahobila Mutt)

Bagavat Sri. Ramanujar   **Sri. Alawandar**

तदेवं मुमुक्षुभिः प्राप्यतया वेदान्तोदित-निरस्तनिखिल अविद्यादिदोषगन्द अनवधिकातिशय असंख्येय कल्याणगुणगण परब्रह्मपुरुषोत्तम प्राप्त्युपायभूत-वेदनोपासनध्यानादि शब्दवाच्य (वाच्यां) तदैकान्तिकात्यन्तिकभक्तिं वक्तुं तदङ्गभूतम् "आत्माऽपहतपाप्मा"(छा.८.७.१)। इत्यादिप्रजापतिवाक्योदितं प्राप्तुरात्मनो याताम्यदर्शनं तन्नित्यताज्ञानपूर्वक असङ्गकर्म निष्षाद्यज्ञानयोगसाध्यमुक्तम् ।

tadēvaṁ mumukṣubhiḥ prāpyatayā vēdāntōdita- nirastanikhila avidyādidōṣaganda anavadhikātiśaya asaṁkhyēya kalyāṇaguṇagaṇa parabrahmapuruṣōttama prāptyupāyabhūta - vēdanōpāsanadhyānādi śabdavācya (vācyāṁ) tadaikāntikātyantikabhaktiṁ vaktuṁ taṅgabhūtam "ātmā'pahatapāpmā"(chā.8.7.1). ityādiprajāpativākyōditaṁ prāpturātmanō yātāmyadarśanaṁ tannityatājñānapūrvaka asaṅgakarma niṣṣādyajñānayōgasādhyamuktam |

Discussions on the PrajApati Vakyam:

Two questions arise in our mind when we read this long sentence.

1.How, what is stated to Arjuna to fight, is applicable to common men like us?

2.How Atma yatatmyam (Atma ShatcatkAram) spoken here (Avara PurushArtam) is applicable to Mumukshus. Is it not that, Parama PurushArtam is to "reach BhagavAn Tiruvadi for Mumukshus". (VishishtAdvaita Philosophy).

Bagavat RamAnujar answers both question in detail in 3rd chapter AvatArikai- of Bagavat GitA

What is stated to Arjuna is not ParamAtmA's Udyeshyam. (Intention) It is only a Vyajyam. (Excuse). In LoukikA what is done for one reason, after the reason is over still continued for Loka Shemam as stated in Brahma SutrA. Similarly, here, even though ArjunA is given Upadesam, it is meant for all of us only.

"Atma YatAtmyam" is an **Angabutam** for realising Bhagavan and that in itself is not PurushArtham.

Both Lord Krishna and Bagavat RamAnujA are trying to say that Gita ShAstram is advocating Bhakti.

And, Bakti **alone** can lead to Brahmam and so, with Love and affection one has to do Bhakti to Him. Swami AlawandAr's summary relating to the entire GitaShAstram is shown in his first slokA of GitArtha Sangragam:

स्वधर्मज्ञानवैराग्यसाध्य भक्त्येक गोचरः |

नारायणः परं ब्रह्म गीता शास्त्रे समीरितः||

svadharmajñānavairāgyasādhyabhaktyēkagōcaraḥ |
nārāyaṇaḥ paraṁ brahma gītā śāstrē samīritaḥ |

(Alawandar-Gitartha Sangraga: slokA-1)

Gita ShAstram is a granta which tells about Bhakti, and Brahmam is Upayam and Upeyam also. (The goal and means) This Bhakti Yoga's Angam is first taught since it is a must to attain His feet, only after realising the **PatyagAtma-**(one's self AtmA) the AngA. This in itself is not a PurushArtam and only a (ladder) step to go up.

Now let us see the full meaning of the sloka mentioned above:

तदेवं मुमुक्षुभि: प्राप्यतया वेदान्तोदित-निरस्तनिखिल अविद्यादिदोषगन्द अनवधिकातिशय असंख्येय कल्याणगुणगण परब्रह्मपुरुषोत्तम प्राप्त्युपायभूत-वेदनोपासनध्यानादि शब्दवाच्य (वाच्यां) तदैकान्तिकात्यन्तिकभक्तिं वक्तुं तदङ्गभूतम् "आत्माऽपहतपाप्मा"(छा.८.७.१)। इत्यादिप्रजापतिवाक्योदितं प्राभुरात्मनो याताम्यदर्शनं तन्नित्यताज्ञानपूर्वक असङ्गकर्म निष्ठाद्यज्ञानयोगसाध्यमुक्तम् ।

Mumuchubhi: - Those who want to get out of SamsAram and do kainkaryam (service) to Brahmam in sarvadesa, sarva kAla, and sarvavastai. These persons also do kainkaryam to Brahmam, in SamsArA. For them what is stated in VedA as PrApyam? Acquirable-i.e., where one must go, which is acquirable by them.

Sri. RamAnujA describes the Brahmam's Lakshanam. (Brahmam is the goal and it is also the means (Route to reach the same).

निरस्तनिखिल अविद्यादिदोषगन्द अनवधिकातिशय असंख्येय कल्याणगुणगण परब्रह्मपुरुषोत्तम प्राप्त्युपायभूत

nirastanikhila avidyādidōṣaganda anavadhikātiśaya asaṁkhyēya kalyāṇaguṇagaṇa parabrahmapuruṣōttama prāptyupāyabhūta.

Brahmam (Sriman NarAyaNA) is unrelated to Avidya dosha etc., (**Dosha Sambandha Anarhan-DoshA never touches Him**) and His KalyANa GuNA are, SwAbAgitvam, (Natural), without any limit, countless, and having Ananda Roopam.

He is addressed as परब्रह्मपुरुषोत्तम- **Parabrahman and PurushOtaman** by Sri. RamAnujA to cover what is stated by both Shruti and Smruti about the supreme reality. Parabrahma is objective name and NarAyaNa is subjective name. PurushOtaman is objective name and Vasudeva is subjective name. He is PrApti UpAyam for Mumukshus. i.e., He is the route-(means) to PrApti for Mumukshus.

6. PrajApati Vakyam- Sri. RamAnujA's explanation

PRAJAPATI VAKYAM- SRI. RAMANUJA'S EXPLANATION ESTABLISHES BRAHMA VIDYA CLEARLY

What should a Mumuks hu do	With desire to leave SamsArA and reach Brahmam's Tiruvadi he must desire and work.	तदेवं मुमुक्षुभिः	tadēvaṁ mumukṣubhiḥ
Who is Brahmam?	Sriman NARAyanA.	परब्रह्म-(Vaidikam) पुरुषोत्तम(Loukikam)	parabrahmapuruṣōttama (Refer above for details)
Who says so?	Refer Sri. Alawandar's sloka above given under GitArtha Sangragam	स्वधर्मज्ञानवैराग्यसाध्य भक्त्येक गोचरः। नारायणः परं ब्रह्म गीता शास्त्रे समीरितः॥	svadharmajñānavairāgyasādhyabhakty ēkagōcaraḥ। nārāyaṇaḥ paraṁ brahma gītā śāstrē samīritaḥ। (Alawandar Gitartha Sangraga: slokA-1)
What are the Brahmam's Lakshanam	KalyANa guNA	निरस्तनिखिल अविद्यादिदोषगन्द अनवधिकातिशय असंख्येय कल्याणगुणगण, प्राप्त्युपायभूत	nirastanikhila avidyādidōṣaganda anavadhikātiśaya asaṁkhyēya kalyāṇaguṇagaṇa, prāptyupāyabhūta

How does a Mumukshhu reach Him?	With desire to leave SamsArA, and reach Brahmam's Tiruvadi he must carry out with Bakti (Love and affection) Vedana, or Dhyanam, or UpAsanam of that single object.	वेदनोपासनध्यानादि शब्दवाच्य (वाच्यां)	vēdanōpāsanadhyānādi śabdavācya (vācyāṁ)
What are the qualities of Bhakti?	Ekantam- By object or PrayojanA (Use) it is Para-Brahmam only, and no one else. (Nirnayam - concluded) Second is always Atyantika- Sarva kAla VyApyam (applicable). This Bhakti on NarAyaNA cannot change with time.	तदैकान्तिकात्यन्तिकभक्तिं वक्तुं	tadaikāntikātyantikabhaktiṁ vaktuṁ
Is this Bhakti and UpAsana sufficient or some more things	PratyagAtma SAtcAtkAram is a must	तदङ्गभूतम् "आत्माऽपहतपाप्मा"(छा.८.७.१)	taṅgabhūtam "ātmā'pahatapāpmā"(chā.8.7.1).

are required?			
Who says so? And when?	PrajApati to DevA king IndrA When Indra sticks to PrajApati and asks questions for route to Liberation.	इत्यादिप्रजापतिवाक्योदितं प्राप्तुरात्मनो यातात्म्यदर्शनं तन्नित्यताज्ञानपूर्वक असङ्गकर्म निष्षाद्यज्ञानयोगसाध्यमुक्तम्	ityādiprajāpativākyōditaṁ prāpturātmanō yātāmyadarśanaṁ tannityatājñānapūrvaka asaṅgakarma niṣṣādyajñānayōgasādhyamuktam

What is advocated in VedA to attain the Brahmam?

वेदनोपासनध्यानादि शब्दवाच्य (वाच्यां), **vēdanōpāsanadhyānādi śabdavācya (vācyāṁ)** i.e., Vedanam (Meditation), UpAsanam, and DhyAnam. All the three are one and the same and so, they are shown separately here. These three are VAcaka sabdham and Bakti is VAchya Sabdham. By following any one of them. **तदैकान्तिकात्यन्तिकभक्तिं वक्तुं**, **tadaikāntikātyantikabhaktiṁ vaktuṁ.** Bakti has two adjectives here. One is **Ekantam**- By object or PrayojanA (Use) Bakti to be expressed to **Para-Brahmam** only and no one else. (Antam-Nirnayam-concluded). Second is **Atyantika**- Sarva kAla VyApyam (applicable). This Bakti is not one time, but continued till one leave this earth.

Before getting such a Bhakti to realise Brahmam, **Sri. RamAnujA** says realising and knowing about Self's AtmA is a must as per **PrajApati Vakyam, in Chandokya Upanishad (8.7.1).** **वक्तुं "आत्माsपहतपाप्मा"(छा.८.७.१)।** **vaktuṁ "ātmā'pahatapāpmā"(chā.8.7.1).** **आत्माsपहतपाप्मा** – refers to a JivA without DoshA. JivA incidentally when attaining MokshA, gets SAmyam with Brahmam for enjoying all the pleasures (Bogams) which He enjoys. Other than Sriyapatitvam, Capacity to make Shrushti and able to give MokshA to JivA, one gets Samyam with Brahmam after attaining MokshA.

By this PrajApati's vAkyam, **"आत्माsपहतपाप्मा"(छा.८.७.१)**, to IndrA who came to PrajApati and asked him to give Upadesam of **"Self-realisation"** it is established that by carrying out Atma ShAtcAtkAram, **whoever wants**

Moksham (liberation), gets GjAnam **(ज्ञानम्)** about Brahman, as a first step, and by Vedana, or Dhyana, or Upasana of that Brahmam, one could then attain MokshA as step-2. *(See also Section 13. Conclusion)*

7. Brahma Vidya according to Wikipedia

Brahmavidya is that branch of scriptural knowledge derived primarily through a study of the Upanishads, Brahma-Sutras and BhagavatGita, and derived from the Sanskrit words Brahma and Vidyā.

Brahmam is the neuter gender of the root word-form "brih" that means big. As the word big has not been further qualified to reveal its dimension, we must understand that Brahmam, the word means that which is free from all forms of limitation.

The word VidyA is derived from the root (Dhatu-in Sanskrit) vid- to know or to learn. To know or learn about Brahmam, only that which helps us to escape, the cycle of birth and death, and attain the feet of the Shrushti Kartha, the Brahmam is VidyA (**Sa VidyA Vimuktaye**) and other learnings or knowledge is only a Loukika Vishayam. (Knowing worldly matters).

Brahmavidya is the spiritual knowledge of the Absolute Truth or Reality or Brahmam according to Brahma-SutrA. Vidya is the highest ideal of classical Sanatana Dharma taught to anyone. Brahma-Vidya does not pertain only to Sanatana Dharma, as many other faiths practice and learn Brahmavidya through different means; Each faith teaches about the divine through different studies, yet the Brahma-Vidya is one and the same – **Truth the Reality itself.**

In the Puranas, this is divided into two branches, the first one dealing with the Vedic mantras and is called Para Vidya or 'former knowledge', and the latter dealing with the study of the Upanishads and is called the Apara-vidya or 'latter knowledge'. Both para- and Apara-vidya constitute Brahma-Vidya. The Mundaka Upanishad says that **"Brahma-vidya sarva-vidya pratistha"**, which means "The Knowledge of Brahman (that which is Brahma is Brahman) is the foundation of all knowledge."

Brahma-mimamsa is a masterly treatise, weighty and illuminating, summing up the Dvaita standpoint in Vedanta by Dharmadhikari Prof., H N Raghanvendrachar, M A., D.O.C., for benefit of readers intrested in Madhvacharya's Dvaita Philosophy.

DhyanA, Meditation and UpAsanA

These three are one and the same. While **meditation** is an English word, **DhyanA** is a Sanskrit word both meaning same. UpAsanA is again a Sanskrit word meaning worship and service. Vedanta Sutras define Upasana as enquiry into Brahman. It does not stop there. It is study, Investigation, and reasoning, contemplation and meditation. Thus, Meditation is long and continued meditation.

8. Adhikari Vishesham, Sources and Knowledge of Brahmam through a Guru

Adhikari Vishesham (Eligibility) for Meditation

A person who is knowledgeable enough to realise that he should act in this Birth itself, to put an end to the cycle of births and deaths becomes eligible for Upasana. It is such a person's love and affection towards Brahmam, that he focuses on Brahman, constantly by meditation. This should not be construed to hinder in daily life, because the daily duties themselves are to be carried out in a spirit of worship of the Lord and with three thyagas namely Kartrutva, Mamata and Phala. (**Kartrutva**- "I" am doing, **Mamata**- Actions and results are Mine, **Phala**- Fruits of actions)

Sources for Brahma Vidya

Upanishads, Vedanta Sutras or Brahma Sutras, and Bhagavat Gita.

In Upanishads, the focus on Brahma Vidya is more under, Chandokya, Bruhadaranyaka, and Taitreeya. Other Upanishads which deal with Brahma Vidya are, Kata Upanishad, Kausheetaki Upanishad, Prasnopanishad, Isavasya Upanishad and Mundaka Upanishad. Some minor changes in numbers are there in the Brahma Vidya. Ramanuja says 32 and Sankara says 30. It does not matter because anyone can choose any Vidya for doing Upasana.

Brahma sutra BhAshyam under chapter three, Padha three, details of Brahma Vidya are dealt with and we will see below the BhAshyam of Sri. RamAnujA briefly. In the introduction of the book, Mundaka and Mandukya Upanishad published by Ramkrishna math, Mylapore, Madras in 1920 and authored by Swami Sharvananda, it is stated that:

The Mundaka Upanishad says that "Brahma-vidya sarva-vidya pratistha", which means **"The Knowledge of Brahman is the foundation of all knowledge."** The book also says that since reference to Mundaka is taken in the name, and Mundaka meaning razor, and shaving head fully, this is more appropriate for Sanyasins than Grahasta.

Knowledge of Brahmam through a Guru

In Sanatana Dharma, Philosophy, all ascetic leaders advocate, the Ultimate goal for the self is Realising Self (Atma), and Brahman as one and the same. But understanding of Self (Atma) or Brahman is a process **guided through a Guru**, who himself has gone through this process of learning from his Guru and reached a stage where he could guide others. All our Scriptures, are therefore always in the form of a Question-and-Answer format only. The Questioner is a great scholar or person, or a King of repute and the Guru is equally or more well versed with knowledge and have experienced to answer their query.

Two, examples are stated here to understand this point: Mahabharat and Ramayana are two Epics (Iti-hasa, this is how it happened), and heroes of both, Yudhistra, and Arjuna, (from Mahabharata) and Rama (from Ramayana) had doubts on purpose of life, and as Kings how they must administer the Kingdom?

Therefore, they asked questions: Yudhistra and Arjuna to Lord Krishna and Rama to Vashishtar. Resultant GranthAs were, **Sri Vishnu Sahasranamam**, (Anushasana Parva Section 149) Bhagavat Gita (does not need any further reference) and **Yoga Vashishtam** (Rama when brought to the Palace for getting instruction from his father to go and help Rishi Viswamittirar at forest, looking at his sadness, Viswamittirar requested Rishi Vashishtar to give him Upadesam about **Paramartika Gjanam, (ज्ञानम्)** (knowledge about Brahman.) The details of questions and answers and what we must follow are all brought out in these Granthas and it would be helpful to understand and lead life according to the advice given in these Grantas, to attain the purpose of Manushya JanmA and to remain happy.

These **Thirty-two VidyAs** are listed below and each one teaches a specific quality(swaroopam) of Brahman on which a Sadaka is supposed to focus constantly and regularly, while carrying out Upasana to achieve liberation. It is also added in this Table extracts from a Tamil book written and published by Dr. Venkatesh MBBs., CCEBDM, MBA. He is a ShishyA of Villur NadAdur, Sri Bhashya SimhAsanam, SAstra SAhitee, Vallaba Vidvanmani, Dr. Sri. MatuPayave, KarunAkarArya Maha Desikan. The name of the book is **Sri Vidyaigalum and Sri. Rajagopalnum**

(ஸ்ரீவித்யைகளும்ஸ்ரீராஜகோபாலனும்.), (மன்னார்குடி ஸ்ரீராஜகோபாலன் செய்தருளியல்லீலைகளும், அவை உணர்த்தும் உபநிஷத் ப்ரஹ்ம வித்யைகளும்). All LeelAs done by BhagavAn Sri. Mannarkudi Rajagopalan and the way they indicate Upanishad Brahma VidyAs.

9. Brahma-Vidya Names

Sr No	Name of the Vidya	Which Upanishad?	What to concentrate in this Vidya	Mannarkudi Rajagopalan Leela.32 Vidyas are shown by Baghavan Kannan to Gopralaya Rishis
1	GAyatri VidyA	Brahman as the Holy Gayatri Mantra	Chandokya Upanishad, III. xii	**Leelais: GopAlan one who mends Cows.** If we do DhyanA of his effulgence, He would control our mind from wandering and stabilise the same as Cows were mended by Him.
2	Aksi(अक्षि) VidyA	Brahman as being present within the Eye	Chandokya Upanishad, IV.xv.1	**Kannan with flute SevA.** Three qualities said in this VidyA, on which to do UpAsanA is shown by Kannan. 1.One who keeps likable objects with Him (SamyAtvAma:) 2.VAmanee: Gives all benefits to those who surrender to Him. 3.Bhamanee: One who has effulgence.
3	AksharAkshara Vidya (**Akshara-Para**)	Meditation on the Imperishable	Mundaka Upanishad, I	**SevA:** सर्वज्ञन्-यसर्वज्ञस्सर्वविद्यस्य ज्ञानमयं तपः One who knows everything clearly by Swaroopam and PrakAram. He made DuryOdanA to stand when He entered the Rajya Sabha. He showed **Sarvagjatvam(सर्वज्ञत्त्वम्)** in this episode.
4	AkAsha VidyA	Making sound and through AkAsha reaches to us.	Chandokya Upanishad-1	**Udgita Sound, though Flute**, by Uth-One who is supreme. Since AkAsha brings all sounds, in this VidyA, ParamAtmA brings this **Utgita** sound to all of us through flute.
5	Sadh-VidyA	Brahman as the ground of all being	Chandokya Upanishad, VI	**VatsApaharaNa sEvA**-During PralayA He alone existed and other Cetana, Acetana (all of them were within Him without name and form). Later after He makes SankalpA to become many they get names and forms. This essence of Sad VidyA was shown by Kannan to Gopralaya Rishis.
6	AntarAdithya VidyA	Brahman as the Inner Controller of the Sun	Chandokya Upanishad, I.vi.6	AntarAdithya VidyA says to do DhyanA of Brahman, **at the center of Surya Mandalam, and with brightness of Gold.** Along with Rukmini, and SatyabhAmA on his crown He sat and gave darshan to Gopralaya Rishis.
7	Bhooma VidyA	Brahman as the Great One	Chandokya Upanishad, VII	Sridevi, Bhudevi sameda **Para Vasudeva sEvA** to Gopralaya Rishis. Bhuma vidya keeps saying one by one which is better than what and finally says Satyam- the ParamAtmA is better

Sr No	Name of the Vidya	Which Upanishad?	What to concentrate in this Vidya	Mannarkudi Rajagopalan Leela.32 Vidyas are shown by Baghavan Kannan to Gopralaya Rishis
				than everyone. This is explained by Bahu+MA- Better than every vastu. Keeping this in mind one l to do DhyanA of Him as recommended by Bhuma VidyA.
8	Madhu VidyA	Brahman as Honey	Chandokya Upanishad, III. i	**Shining in like SuryA**-Without UdayA (rising) and AstamaNA (To go away) ParaBrahmam is always shining in like SuryA as stated in this VidyA. This sEvA was shown to Yashoda when He drank milk from her Breast.
9	Purusha VidyA	Milkman SevA to show that milk is important for YagA and JivA's life itself is a YagA.	Chandokya Upanishad, III. 16,17	**Milk man** -पुरुष वाव यज्ञः This VidyA says the life of a Jiva itself is a YAgA. Since the life itself is depicted as a YagA, He takes the form of a milk man and showed milk is an important Dravyam for YagA.

Sr No	Name of the Vidya	Which Upanishad?	What to concentrate in this Vidya	Mannarkudi Rajagopalan Leela.32 Vidyas are shown by Baghavan Kannan to Gopralaya Rishis
10	SarvAntarAtmaVidyA	BhagavAn is AntarAtmA for everyone.	Brahadaranyam Upanishad-111-7	**Vatsa-KapitsAsura Vadam**-यं पृथिवी न वेद, यस्य पृथिवी शरीरं, यः पृथिवीं अन्तरो यमयति, in this VidyA, starts like this and says Earth, water, Agni (Fire) and AkAsham all are His shareeram and He remains within them as **AntarAtmA.** Further He even stays inside JivA is stated in this Upanishad. य आत्मनि तिष्ठन्, आत्मनो sन्तरः, यमात्मा न वेद, यस्यआत्माशरीरं, यआत्मानं अन्तरो यमयति, एष त आत्मा अन्तर्याम्यमृतः
11	VysvAnara VidyA	Brahman as the Universal Being. Viswaroopa Darshanam	Chandokya Upanishad, V. xi	**GitAUpadesam-Viswaroopa Darshanam.** VysvAnara Vidya describes the **Viswaroopa Darshanam as follows:** तस्यहवाएतस्यातमनःड
12	PanchAgni VidyA	The Meditation of the Five Fires	Chandokya Upanishad, V. iii to x.	A JivA's **sooskhama ShreerA** along with PrANA and Senses (IndriyA) is first joined with "Swarga Agni." Second is "Megam

Sr No	Name of the Vidya	Which Upanishad?	What to concentrate in this Vidya	Mannarkudi Rajagopalan Leela.32 Vidyas are shown by Baghavan Kannan to Gopralaya Rishis
				Agni". Third in "Bhumi Agni, "Fourth into mens" shareerA. Last and fifth is Stree's shareerA, stays there for ten months and then born in this earth. Therefore, it becomes a PancAgni VidyA. Similar to giving Ahuti with DravyA in Agni, if one gives his AtmA in PancAgni He will take the JivA to Moksha through ArchirAdi Gati. Since **ButanA, gave her milk from Stanam, having kept it as ArpaNam to Him only she attained MokshA.**
13	Dahara VidyA	Brahman as the Imperceptible Ether within the Heart	Chandokya Upanishad, VIII	**Rukmani, SatyabHAma Sri Rajagopalan SevA.** Dahara Vidya advocates, a UpAsakan's ShareerA as Brahmapuram, (Brahmam's place of residence), and the Lotus at the center of the Heart as His residence, shrinking all His greatness, Brahmam resides in the small place inside heart of a JivA. That Brahmam is to be searched and found. Dahara Vidya says find out such a Brahman inside you.
14	PrAna VidyA	Brahman as the Vital Breath	Chandokya Upanishad, I.xi.5	**SevA in Haridra River in Mannarkudi,** along with GopikA (jalakridA). PrAna. This Vidya explains PrAna's greatness and explains the method to do UpAsanaA of Brahmam, residing within that PrAna as AntarAtmA. The way we cannot live without PrAna, GopikAs showed they cannot live with their PrAnanAthan Kannan.
15	NachiketAgni VidyA	Meditation with the Naciketa fire	Katha Upanishad, I. ii	**NachketAgni.** NachiketA goes to the God of death's place. (Yamadharma RajA's kingdom). NachiketA gets three boons from YamA out of which second boon is "NachketA's query about Agni which takes to SwargA (Here SwargA is MokshA) YamA also gave him a boon and named the second Agni as NachketAgni. Meditation on that Agni leads to SwargA to be understood as Liberation.
16	Upakosala VidyA	Meditation as taught to Upakosala-	Chandokya Upanishad, IV. x	**Rukmani-SatyabhAmA sevA and listening to flute songs.** कं ब्रह्म खं ब्रह्म. कं is bliss and खं is limitless. This shows that Brahmam

Sr No	Name of the Vidya	Which Upanishad?	What to concentrate in this Vidya	Mannarkudi Rajagopalan Leela.32 Vidyas are shown by Baghavan Kannan to Gopralaya Rishis
				is without limits, and like AkAshA limitless with AnandA. It is to show that limitless AnandA he gave SevA to us as **Rukmani-SatyabhAmA sameda GopAlan listening to flute.**
17	SatyakAma VidyA	Meditation as taught to Satyakaama Jaabaala	Chandokya Upanishad, IV. iv	In this Vidya, Brahmam showed four different SevA to a person named SatyakAman as Bull or Ox, Agni, Annam, and a Bird named Madugu. In this each one said how Brahmam looks. Bullock said Brahmam have four different RoopA. First one Bull said, having East, West, South and North direction within Brahmam. Second, Agni said, Buloka, SwarlogA, Antariksha LogA and Ocean within Brahmam. Third, an Annam said, Agni, Sun, Chandran, Lightening within Brahmam. Fourth and last a bird said, PrANA, Eyes, ears, and Manas within Brahmam. In this way just as Brahmam is divided into four different forms and shown to SatyakAman, Kannan showed to GopikAs four different forms as **YamA to Boxers, King, for GopikA and PrajA, and all three in one form to Gopila GopralayA.**

Sr No	Name of the Vidya	Which Upanishad?	What to concentrate in this Vidya	Mannarkudi Rajagopalan Leela.32 Vidyas are shown by Baghavan Kannan to Gopralaya Rishis

Sr No	Name of the Vidya	Which Upanishad?	What to concentrate in this Vidya	Mannarkudi Rajagopalan Leela.32 Vidyas are shown by Baghavan Kannan to Gopralaya Rishis
18	IsAvAshya VidyA	GovardhanaGiri dHari sEvA	IsAvAshya (ईशावास्य) SlokA-II	**GovardhanaGiri dHari sEvA** **ईशवास्यं इदं सर्वम्.** Kannan said to Ayars (ஆயர்கள்) that He resides in everything in this Universe, and so, do PoojA to Govardhana Giri. He was inside the Giri as AntaryAmi and took that PoojA. Also, this Upanishad teaches NishkAmya karma. He stopped Ayars from doing Indra PoojA and made them do PoojA to Govardhana Giri as an angam of His tiruvArAdhaNa

Sr No	Name of the Vidya	Which Upanishad?	What to concentrate in this Vidya	Mannarkudi Rajagopalan Leela.32 Vidyas are shown by Baghavan Kannan to Gopralaya Rishis
				... समाः । एवं त्वयि नान्यथेतोऽस्ति न कर्म लिप्यते नरे ।।
19	Samvarga VidyA	The entire Universe inside His mouth to YashOdhA.	Chandokya Upanishad, IV. iii	**The entire Universe inside His mouth to YashOdhA** Vayu and PrANA, both are shareerA for Brahmam is shown. In this way Sun, Moon, Agni, Eyes, Ears, and Manas everything is within Brahmam is seen by YashOdhA. By opening His mouth and showing her the entire Universe, the point is everything is within Him.
20	Gargi-Akshara VidyA	Brahman as the support for everything.	Brhadaaranyaka Upanishad, III.viii.8	**With stick in His hand, he is mending all Cows SevA.** Yagjnyavalkar says to Gargi, Brahmam which is support (AdhAram) for everything is named as Aksharam, in this VidyA.**एतद्वै तदक्षरं गार्गी ब्राह्मणा अभिवदन्ति.** Further Yagjnyavalkar says to Gargi, that only due to His (Brahmam) SankalpA Sun, Moon, Bhumi, and AkAshA are all carrying out their KarmA-actions in their respective places. This is shown by Kannan with stick in His hand and mending all the Cows. By seeing the stick only, they all move, and by this He showed that entire Universe do their activity only by His sankalpA.
21	Bhrugu-Varuni VidyA	Meditation as taught by the god Varuna	Taittiriya Upanishad, Bhriguvalli	**Kannan as child crawling to YashOdhA SevA.** Bhrugu Muni asks VaruNA, to make him know Brahmam. VaruNA replied him to start thinking with his Intellect and know Him. Bhrugu also did the same and Taitreeya Upanishad says, finally Bhrugu understood that Brahmam is Ananda Roopam. (प्राणो ब्रह्मेति व्यजानात्, मनो ब्रह्मेति व्यजानात्, आनन्दं ब्रह्मेति व्यजानात्)
22	Anandamaya-VidyA	Brahman as the Self consisting of Bliss	Taittiriya Upanishad, Anandavalli	**Playing with GopikA in a park with extreme happiness SevA.** Brahmam's Anandam is one hundred times more than BrahmA, but it continues to say with our Manas we cannot understand the same. The essence of Ananda maya VidyA as per Anandavalli in Taitreeya Upanishad is not only He enjoys, but makes His BhaktA also equally enjoy.

Sr No	Name of the Vidya	Which Upanishad?	What to concentrate in this Vidya	Mannarkudi Rajagopalan Leela.32 Vidyas are shown by Baghavan Kannan to Gopralaya Rishis
23	AngushtamAtra-VidyA	Brahman as resident within the Heart, of individual, of the size of Thumb	Katha Upanishad, II.iv.12	Even though Brahmam is boundary and limitless, He shrinks Himself **to the size of every individual AtmA's thumb size and present in their heart** for them to see and do UpAsanA says, KathA Upanishad. In order to show that He could shrink and show Himself to His BaktA, **He Himself got tied to Ural(உரல்) and shown His SevA to YashOdhA.** But the doshA in them does not touch Him and He also does not hate them because of their Asuddhi in ShareerA or DoshA. अङ्गुष्ठमात्रःपुरुषोमध्यआत्मनितिष्ठति। ईशानोभूतभव्यस्य न ततो विजुगुप्सते ॥
24	ShAndilya-VidyA	Meditation as taught by Sandilya	Chandokya Upanishad, III.xiv.7	**Brahmam shows Himself differently to those who are proud and those who are having Bakti with affection to Him.** When He is inside our heart, He is even smaller than $1/100^{th}$ of the tip of the paddy, but we know He is biggest of all (ब्रह्म). This is the essence of ShAndilya-VidyA. This is the SevA he showed to Rukmani satisfying Himself with a Tulsi Leaf and for SatyabhAmA even when She put all Her ornaments, did not allow the weighing scale to tilt in favour of ornaments.

Sr No	Name of the Vidya	Which Upanishad?	What to concentrate in this Vidya	Mannarkudi Rajagopalan Leela.32 Vidyas are shown by Baghavan Kannan to Gopralaya Rishis
25	Balaki -VidyA	Meditation as taught to Baalaaki	Kaushitaki Upanishad, IV	Kalia Nardhana SevA. Kalian thought Kannan was a child and surrounded his body and tried to kill Him. But when **Kannan, stood on Kalian's head**, he realised that He must be Brahmam Sriman NarAyaNA. Kaushitaki Upanishad teaches this Vidya यो वे बालाके एतेषां पुरुषाणां कर्ता, यस्य वैतत् कर्म, स वै वेदितव्यः that Brahmam is karthA and Cause for everything, and He is the one we must know. (**Vid-VidyA**). This Upanishad further says, if a JivA

Sr No	Name of the Vidya	Which Upanishad?	What to concentrate in this Vidya	Mannarkudi Rajagopalan Leela.32 Vidyas are shown by Baghavan Kannan to Gopralaya Rishis
				understands/knows) that Brahmam is the cause and KarthA for everything and does UpAsanA of Him, He removes all his KarmA and gives him Moksha (which is a higher state than a SamsAri and belongs to Brahmam)
26	Ushastha-Kahola-VidyA	Dancing child with butter on one hand.	Brhadaaranyaka Upanishad, II. iv, v	**Dancing child with butter on one hand SevA.** Essence of Ushastha-Kahola-VidyA is: We can also live with Anandam of a child, after attaining MokshA through Him, when we realise, and do UpAsanA of Him, that Brahmam is inside every Atma, similar to butter being inside Milk. एषत आत्मा सर्वान्तरोऽतोऽन्यदार्तम् तस्मात् ब्राह्मणः पाण्डित्यं निर्विद्य बाल्येन तिष्ठासेत्
27	Maitreyi-VidyA	Meditation as taught by Yajnavalkya to his wife Maitreyi	Brhadaaranyaka Upanishad, II. iv	Rukmani-SatyabhAmA sameda SevA Maitryi Vidya teaches, "आत्मा वा अरे द्रष्टव्यः श्रोतव्यो मन्तव्यो निदित्यासितव्यः" In this Vidya there are only **two commands**, which are one has **to see Brahmam as if he is seeing Him in person,** (द्रष्टव्यः) and carry out DhyAnam of Him (निदित्यासितव्यः) along with Rukmini and SatyabhAmA (single-as a Vishishta vidhi) as per our AchAryAs. Other vAkyams श्रोतव्यः, मन्तव्यः are not commands, since one who learns VedA will automatically listen to the same and think about it in mind. These are recitation or repetitions.
28	Parama-Purusha-VidyA	Brahman as the Supreme Person. He is the means and He is the Goal also.	Katha Upanishad, I. iii	DasAvatAra sevA to DadhipAndavan, since he gave place to hide to Lord Krishna, when YashodA was running after Him to beat Him due to His stealing Curd. He requested Kannan, to give him mokshA as a pratiupakAram. **This VidyA teaches that DadhipAndavan, was not fit for UpAyam, the Bhakti YogA and so, Brahmam (Kannan) Himself stood as (UpAyam) means and gave him and his pot mokshA.**

Sr No	Name of the Vidya	Which Upanishad?	What to concentrate in this Vidya	Mannarkudi Rajagopalan Leela.32 Vidyas are shown by Baghavan Kannan to Gopralaya Rishis
				बुद्धिं तु सारथीं विद्द,मनः प्रग्रहं एव च, इन्द्रियाणि ह्यान् आहुः Brahmam is the ultimate goal a JivA has to attain and aim for is brought out in this VidyA. This Upanishad under Paramapurusha vidyA, says, AtmA as traveller in the chariot, body is chariot, Buddhi (intellect) is charioteer, Mind (manas) is bridle, and senses are horses. सोऽध्वनः पारमाप्नोति तद्विष्णोः परमं पदम्) Brahmam is the ultimate goal a JivA has to attain and aim for. सा काष्ठा सा परा गतिः Upanishad also says, the goal (Upeyam) and means (UpAyam) both are Brahmam only.
29	Paryanka-VidyA	Brahman as the highest God seated in the Supreme Abode	Kaushitaki Upanishad, I	SevA: Kannan as MadanagopAlan, embraces all the GopikAs with affection and Love. In this VidyA it is stated that, those MuktAtmA who reach VaikuntA, Brahmam takes them in His lap, and give them BrahmAnubhavam and limitless Anandam. This is the essence of this Paryanka VidyA also.

Sr No	Name of the Vidya	Which Upanishad?	What to concentrate in this Vidya	Mannarkudi Rajagopalan Leela.32 Vidyas are shown by Baghavan Kannan to Gopralaya Rishis
30	JyothishAmjyotir-VidyA	Brahman as the Light of Lights	Brhadaaranyaka Upanishad, IV. iii.	SevA: Eating with GopikAs. अत्र पिताऽपिताभवति,माताऽमाता,लोकाऽलोका,देवाऽदेवाः GopikAs, forgetting their parents, residence, and city and in stoon stage enjoy and eat with Brahmam, (Kannan). In this vidyA, Rishi, Yagjnyavalkar teaches King JanakA, about JivA, uniting with Brahmam in sleeping state. This VidyA explains, the JivA in sleeping state as follows: प्राज्ञेनात्मना संपरिष्वक्त्तो न बाह्यं किंचन वेद नान्तरम्।

Sr No	Name of the Vidya	Which Upanishad?	What to concentrate in this Vidya	Mannarkudi Rajagopalan Leela.32 Vidyas are shown by Baghavan Kannan to Gopralaya Rishis
				शोकान्तरम् ॥ During the sleeping state of JivA, the Brahmam embraces him and makes him not to have any sorrow and keeps him in a state of Anandam (Bliss)
31	NyAsa-VidyA	Self-surrender to Brahmam	Taittiriya Upanishad - II	**SevA:** GopikAstree Raining their hands and making SaraNAgati to Brahmam-Kannan to give back their dresses. Essence of NyAsa VidyA is to surrender completely to Brahmam, and enter-into His Kainkaryam (SevA- serve Him in all possible ways) न्यास इत्याहुर्मनीषिणो ब्रह्माणं ब्रह्मा विश्वः कतमः स्वयम्भुः प्राजपतिः संवत्सर इति । This Vidya says, NyAsa, the surrender to Brahmam is the highest form of everything one could do. To leave surrender, and submit to Him all our responsibilities and burden (भार) is NyAsa.
32	Pratardhana VidyA	Meditation as taught to Pratardana by the god Indra to meditate on Brahman as AntayAmi (soul) of IndrA.	Kaushitaki Upanishad, III	**PrANA** as ParamatmA Himself. Kaushitaki Upanishad declares that PrANA is life and immortality and one's life span depends on it. Therefore, through meditating PrANA one attains immortality. The Upanishad says selves are supported and held by PrANA. PrANA is Atman, and therefore one should meditate on it. In the VedAnta Sutra 1.1.24 is described as very cause of origination and destruction of all things in the Universe and hence connotes the Brahmam Himself. Between senses and PrANA there was a competition as to who is supreme? It is seen that one of the IndriyAs stopped working, others continued to function, while when PrANA left all other senses departed from the ShreerA.

10. How do we Liberate ourselves from the cycle of birth and death?

While doing ones' Swadharma (Karma,) with **Kartrutva, Mamata and Phala Thyaga,** (As stated by Lord Krishna in many slokas in Bagavat GitA) and simultaneously strive for Liberation (Relief from Samsara-End of Cycle of birth and death). There is huge volume of Literature available in Sanatana Dharma, which we must understand by learning from a Guru, and reading those books published by various authors through many publishing houses, and other specialists on VedAntA field of study. Therefore, **this understanding of Self, and Brahman, their Lakshanams, (GuNA-Attributes) and relation between them, through a Guru, and carrying out Upasana, of that Brahmam with His Kalyana Gunas, is the essence of any Brahma VidyA.**

It is stated in Upanishads and Veda Poorvangam i.e., Poorva Mimasa (Karma Kandam,) that through this Manushya Shreeram only, one could attain this knowledge, since Buddhi is given to Manushya Janma only. With the help of Buddhi, one understands the Dos and Donts of Shruti, (ShastrA) and Smruti (Itihasa, Purana etc.,) and knows the purpose of this Manushya Janma is **only** to liberate one-self from the Cycle of Birth and Death. As one progresses in learning he also has to **service to the Society, as stipulated in Subhashitani** (Collection of many advises given by Rishis) and Meditation on Brahman.

परोपकारायफलन्ति वृक्षाः परोपकाराय वहन्तिनद्यः ।

परोपकाराय दुहन्ति गावः परोपकारार्थमिदं शरीरम् ॥

parōpakārāyaphalanti vṛkṣāḥ parōpakāraya vahantinadyaḥ ।

parōpakāraya duhanti gāvaḥ parōpakārārthamidaṁ śarīram ॥

Trees give fruits for others, rivers flow for others, Cows give Milk for others. Likewise, this human body (ShareerA) of ours is for the service of others. Just as Trees will not eat fruits itself, rivers will not drink water herself, cows will not drink milk herself, our body is also for the service of others and not just for ourselves.

Out of the famous "Trio, of Vedanta namely Upanishads, Brahma Sutra, and Bhagavat Gita, first two shows us clearly thirty-two such Brahma VidyAs, leading us to the supreme Brahmam. Some of them, show us the ways to attain worldly benefits or goods also. **These thirty-two VidyAs show us the path of Upasana, (Meditation), and worship with utmost faith.**

"NyAsa-VidyA" is proclaimed as the excellent one by Itihasas, Puranas, and Agamas. Nyasa is called by various names, viz Prapatti, Bharanyasa, Nikshepa, and Sharanagati. According to this VidyA complete surrender to Brahmam, with full faith and conviction, to serve Him eternally and that believe in His capability to give Liberation and save us from all calamities and Mrutyu. (Rakshakatvam). It demands a life, in full agreement with Shastra, and carrying out one's Swadharma, with three thyaga referred above, promising liberation at the end of one's life time itself (or as wished and prayed by a Jiva).

11. Gayatri examples of Brahma Vidya from Upanishads

Gayatri Vidya: (Chandokya Upanishad- 3-12-1)

पूर्णमप्रवर्तनीं श्रियं लभते य एवं वेद

pūrṇāmapravartanīṁ śriyaṁ labhatē ya ēvaṁ vēda

Gayatri VidyA says, that if one equates Brahman and Gayatri Mantram equally and does Brahmopasanam, he attains wealth which does not leave him.

Gayatri VidyA also says:

गायत्री वा इदं सर्वं भूतं यदिदं किंच। वाग्वै गायत्री। वाग्वा इदं सर्वं भूतं गायति च त्रायते च ॥

gāyatrī vā idaṁ sarvaṁ bhūtaṁ yadidaṁ kiṁca. vāgvai gāyatrī. vāgvā idaṁ sarvaṁ bhūtaṁ gāyati ca trāyatē ca

Whatever we see around is Gayatree only, that itself is Vakku, (speech), that sings, and the same is protecting us. Gayatri is Brahman Himself.

12. Brahma VidyA rules in Brahma Sutram: (साधन-उपासन-अध्यायम्-IIIᵈअध्यायम्)

1. In all the thirty two VidyAs the Vidhi, one who is to be taken into DhyAnam, Name of the deity, Roopam etc are all united meaning same and so, they are all ONE VidyA only.

2. Only if Roopam changes, VidyA will change.

3. In Kausheetaki and Chandokya VidyA, PrANa Vidya is same.

4. AnanDAdhi, Swaroopa, Niroopaka DharmAs are to be followed in all VidyAs.

5. Acamana water before and after Bojanam (Eating) is to be treated as Vastram (dress) for PrANA.

6. ShAndilya VidyA stated in both places are same.

7. Aditya mandalam and eyes, (in both these places,) Brahmam's swaroopam is different even though PrANa shareerA and so, to be done UpAsanam separately or differently.

8. AkAsha VyApti also, is to be followed in all places except where they are projected as alpapradesam.

9. Because of Roopa Bedam, what is stated in Taitreeya and Chandokya Upanishads are different.

10. SamnO mitra: etc., are not VidyAs. They are AngA for Upanishads

11. One who leaves for Moksha, leaves behind him his PunyA to friends and Papa to Enemys is to be understood.

12. Before a Mumukshu and UpAsakan, leaves for ArchirAdi mArgA, all his PunyA and PavA must be got rid off.

13. All UPAsaakAs travel through ArchirAdi MArgA only.

14. Nir doshA and, kalyANa GuNA are applicable to all VidyAs.

15. Ushashti Kaholar's question asks many questions. But the answer is one only.i.e., SarvantarAtmA is the deity to be done UpAsanam.

16. vajasaneyagam and Chandokya Dahara VidyAs are same.

17. UdgitopAsana is not YagjnA Angam for Dahara Vidya's.

18. Dahara UpAsanam is to be done with GuNAshtakam, and satyavAdi Swaroopam.

19. NArAyaNAnuvakam establishes that what is seen in other VidyAs, the deity Indra, SivA etc SabdhAs only point to NarAyaNA.

20. Vag-chit and Manas-chit are told, to get VidyAmayakratu siddhi only

21. In ParavIdyA, Brahmam is to be prayed with Special attribute of Brahmam-namely JivAtmA Apahata-PApma

22. Udgita UpAsanA is applicable to all VidyAs.

23. In VaisvAnara VidyA, all AvayavAs are to be included while doing UpAsanA.

24. GuNA and Vidhi where different VidyAs are different.

25. PhalA for all VidyAs are one only and so, it is enough to carry out one VidyA only.

IVth Padam: फलाध्यायम्

1. Karmas are angam of UpAsanam and not otherwise.

2. Udgita UpAsanam is to be done with Rasatamam

3. Swataketu's UpAkyAnAdis are for stotra of each VidyA and not stories.

4. Sanyasis are AdhikAris for UpAsanA with their DharmAs.

5. VidyAs are to follow YagjnAdi KarmAs.

6. Those who do YagjnA also must have Sama, Dama attributes.

7. If in emergency (when death like situation arise) UpAsakA can take any food.

8. AngAs for uPAsanA, like YagjnA are applicable to Asrama dharmA also. Widowers are also eligible for DhAna, Japa UpAsanams.

9. Those who do not follow Ashrama dharmA are not eligible for UpAsanA.

10. Udgita etc., which are angams of Vidya are to be carried out by Ruthviks (those who have done VedadyAnam)

11. It is very essential for UpAsakAs, to have cintana of Divya Mangala Vigraham.

12. UpAsakan should not speak about his prides to others.

13. BrahmopAsanam, if not hindered by popular karma, gives immediate PhalA.

14. BrahmopAsanam for Mukti might not give immediate PhalA.

15. UpAsam is to be done entire life quite often.

16. UpAsakan has to assume Brahmam as his AtmA, while doing UpAsanam.

17. Manas etc., very low placed while doing UpAsanam has to be taken as highest Deity.

18. Keep Aditya Buddhi in UdgitA.

19. UpAsanam to be done while sitting only.

20. Once Vidya, starts to give phalan, the earlier PavA will go away and latter ones will not stick.

21. PunyA done before and after VidyA will not stick also.

22. Karma, not started giving effects will only burn.

23. Without expectation of PhalA, Nitya and Naimittika Karmas to be carried out compulsorily.

24. PrArabda Karma, need not vanish in One birth and one ShareerA

॥ ब्रह्मविद्योपनिषत् ॥

॥ BRAHMAVIDYOPANIṢAT ॥

स्वाविद्यातत्कार्यजातं यद्विद्यापह्नवं गतम् ।
तद्धंसविद्यानिष्पन्नं रामचन्द्रपदं भजे ॥

svāvidyātatkāryajātaṃ yadvidyāpahnavaṃ gatam |

taddhaṃsavidyāniṣpannaṃ rāmacandrapadaṃ bhaje ॥

ॐ सह नाववतु ॥ सह नौ भुनक्तु ॥

oṃ saha nāvavatu ॥ saha nau bhunaktu ॥

सह वीर्यं करवावहै ॥

saha vīryaṃ karavāvahai ॥

तेजस्विनावधीतमस्तु मा विद्विषावहै ॥

tejasvināvadhītamastu mā vidviṣāvahai ॥

ॐ शान्तिः शान्तिः शान्तिः ॥

oṃ śāntiḥ śāntiḥ śāntiḥ ॥

अथ ब्रह्मविद्योपनिषदुच्यते ॥

atha brahmavidyopaniṣaducyate ॥

प्रसादाद्ब्रह्मणस्तस्य विष्णोरद्भुतकर्मणः ।
रहस्यं ब्रह्मविद्याया ध्रुवाग्निं सम्प्रचक्षते ॥ १॥

prasādādbrahmaṇastasya viṣṇoradbhutakarmaṇaḥ |

rahasyaṃ brahmavidyāyā dhruvāgniṃ sampracakṣate ॥ 1 ॥

ॐइत्येकाक्षरं ब्रह्म यदुक्तं ब्रह्मवादिभिः ।

शरीरं तस्य वक्ष्यामि स्थानं कालत्रयं तथा ॥ २॥

oṃityekākṣaraṃ brahma yaduktaṃ brahmavādibhiḥ ।

śarīraṃ tasya vakṣyāmi sthānaṃ kālatrayaṃ tathā ॥ 2॥

तत्र देवास्त्रयः प्रोक्ता लोका वेदास्त्रयोऽग्नयः ।

तिस्रो मात्रार्धमात्रा च त्र्यक्षरस्य शिवस्य तु ॥ ३॥

tatra devāstrayaḥ proktā lokā vedāstrayo'gnayaḥ ।

tisro mātrārdhamātrā ca tryakṣarasya śivasya tu ॥ 3॥

SLOKA 1-3

The indication of the Brahman, by the PranavA, which contains the

secret significance of Brahma VidyA.

After one has acquired the requisite attainmnets to know Brahma VidyA, he is initiated into Brahma Vidyopanishad for his benefit. By the grace of Brahman (Vishnu), the steady fire, which reduces to ashes the ignorance, the truth underlying Brahma VidyA is, the Brahman. It is stated here the monosyllable "Om" is the Brahman. Now we will relate, what is it's Body, it's seat and three durations. They are three DevAs, three worlds, the three VedAs, three fires, and the three Matras and the half Matra (syllable) of the three lettered ShivA.

ऋग्वेदो गार्हपत्यं च पृथिवी ब्रह्म एव च ।

आकारस्य शरीरं तु व्याख्यातं ब्रह्मवादिभिः ॥ ४॥

ṛgvedo gārhapatyaṃ ca pṛthivī brahma eva ca ।

ākārasya śarīraṃ tu vyākhyātaṃ brahmavādibhiḥ ॥ 4॥

यजुर्वेदोऽन्तरिक्षं च दक्षिणाग्निस्तथैव च ।
विष्णुश्च भगवान्देव उकारः परिकीर्तितः ॥ ५ ॥

yajurvedo'ntarikṣaṃ ca dakṣiṇāgnistathaiva ca ।
viṣṇuśca bhagavāndeva ukāraḥ parikīrtitaḥ ॥ 5 ॥

सामवेदस्तथा द्यौश्चाहवनीयस्तथैव च ।
ईश्वरः परमो देवो मकारः परिकीर्तितः ॥ ६ ॥

sāmavedastathā dyauścāhavanīyastathaiva ca ।
īśvaraḥ paramo devo makāraḥ parikīrtitaḥ ॥ 6 ॥

सूर्यमण्डलमध्येऽथ ह्यकारः शङ्खमध्यगः ।
उकारश्चन्द्रसंकाशस्तस्य मध्ये व्यवस्थितः ॥ ७ ॥

sūryamaṇḍalamadhye'tha hyakāraḥ śaṅkhamadhyagaḥ ।
ukāraścandrasaṃkāśastasya madhye vyavasthitaḥ ॥ 7 ॥

मकारस्त्वग्निसंकाशो विधूमो विद्युतोपमः ।
तिस्रो मात्रास्तथा ज्ञेया सोमसूर्याग्निरूपिणः ॥ ८ ॥

makārastvagnisaṃkāśo vidhūmo vidyutopamaḥ ।
tisro mātrāstathā jñeyā somasūryāgnirūpiṇaḥ ॥ 8 ॥

शिखा तु दीपसंकाशा तस्मिन्नुपरि वर्तते ।
अर्धमात्र तथा ज्ञेया प्रणवस्योपरि स्थिता ॥ ९ ॥

śikhā tu dīpasaṃkāśā tasminnupari vartate ।
ardhamātra tathā jñeyā praṇavasyopari sthitā ॥ 9 ॥

The body of the **"अ-A"**, of the Pranava, as stated in RgvedA, the Garhapatya fire, the earth and God Brahman.

The **"उ-U"** of the Pranava, as stated in Yajurveda, Antariksha (the middle world), Dakshina Fire and Lord Vishnu.

The **"म्-M"** of the Pranava, as stated in Samaveda, and Swarga loka (upper region), the Ahavaniya fire, and Para Brahman IswarA.

The three Matra syllable are similarly to be understood, as one of the forms of the Moon, Sun, and the Fire. Even as the flame of the lam stands over it, so also should the ArdhamAtrA to be understood, as   standing over the Pranava

पद्मसूत्रनिभा सूक्ष्मा शिखा सा दृश्यते परा ।
सा नाडी सूर्यसंकाशा सूर्यं भित्त्वा तथापरा ॥ १०॥

padmasūtranibhā sūkṣmā śikhā sā dṛśyate parā |
sā nāḍī sūryasaṃkāśā sūryaṃ bhittvā tathāparā ॥ 10॥

द्विसप्ततिसहस्राणि नाडीं भित्त्वा च मूर्धनि ।
वरदः सर्वभूतानां सर्वं व्याप्यावतिष्ठति ॥ ११॥

dvisaptatisahasrāṇi nāḍīṃ bhittvā ca mūrdhani |
varadaḥ sarvabhūtānāṃ sarvaṃ vyāpyāvatiṣṭhati ॥ 11॥

*Breaking through the Nadis and the Sun by bringing
Susumna to bear on them*

The transcendent (Sushumna) flame is seen to be as subtle as the fibre of the Lotus-stalk. The transcendent Nadi, resembling the Sun and bursting through the Sun and similarly bursting as under the 72000 Nadis, pervading all, stands in the head as if he is giver of the boons to all beings.

कांस्यघण्टानिनादस्तु यथा लीयति शान्तये ।
ओङ्कारस्तु तथा योज्यः शान्तये सर्वमिच्छता ॥ १२॥

kāṃsyaghaṇṭāninādastu yathā līyati śāntaye |
oṅkārastu tathā yojyaḥ śāntaye sarvamicchatā || 12||

यस्मिन्विलीयते शब्दस्तत्परं ब्रह्म गीयते ।
धियं हि लीयते ब्रह्म सोऽमृतत्वाय कल्पते ॥ १३॥

yasminvilīyate śabdastatparaṃ brahma gīyate |
dhiyaṃ hi līyate brahma so'mṛtatvāya kalpate || 13||

*Attainment of liberation by the Laya aur or dissolution
of the of the sound of the Pranava*

That Yogin who dissolves his inner sense (that is Manas-the Mind) along with the sound of PranavA of sixteen MAtrAs, attains oneness with Brahman, giving up the delusion of existence apart from the Atman. (This is Advaitic concept). Atma-SamarpaNam is done with PraNavA alone according to ShAstrA.

वायुः प्राणस्तथाकाशस्त्रिविधो जीवसंज्ञकः ।
स जीवः प्राण इत्युक्तो वालाग्रशतकल्पितः ॥ १४॥

vāyuḥ prāṇastathākāśastrividho jīvasaṃjñakaḥ ।

sa jīvaḥ prāṇa ityukto vālāgraśatakalpitaḥ ॥ 14॥

नाभिस्थाने स्थितं विश्वं शुद्धतत्त्वं सुनिर्मलम् ।
आदित्यमिव दीप्यन्तं रश्मिभिश्चाखिलं शिवम् ॥ १५॥

nābhisthāne sthitaṃ viśvaṃ śuddhatattvaṃ sunirmalam ।

ādityamiva dīpyantaṃ raśmibhiścākhilaṃ śivam ॥ 15॥

Exposition of the real form of the jiva

That which is Called the JivA, is Vital air (PrAnA), radiance and the ether. The JivA is known as PrANA which is made of one-hundredth part of the awn of a grain of wild paddy.

सकारं च हकारं च जीवो जपति सर्वदा ।

नाभिरन्ध्राद्विनिष्क्रान्तं विषयव्याप्तिवर्जितम् ॥ १६॥

sakāraṃ ca hakāraṃ ca jīvo japati sarvadā ।

nābhirandhrādviniṣkrāntaṃ viṣayavyāptivarjitam ॥ 16॥

तेनेदं निष्कलं विद्यात्क्षीरात्सर्पिर्यथा तथा ।

कारणेनात्मना युक्तः प्राणायामैश्च पञ्चभिः ॥ १७॥

tenedaṃ niṣkalaṃ vidyātkṣīrātsarpiryathā tathā |

kāraṇenātmanā yuktaḥ prāṇāyāmaiśca pañcabhiḥ ‖ 17‖

चतुष्कला समायुक्तो भ्राम्यते च हृदिस्थितः ।

गोलकस्तु यदा देहे क्षीरदण्डेन वा हतः ॥ १८॥

catuṣkalā samāyukto bhrāmyate ca hṛdisthitaḥ |

golakastu yadā dehe kṣīradaṇḍena vā hataḥ ‖ 18‖

एतस्मिन्वसते शीघ्रमविश्रान्तं महाखगः ।

यावन्निश्वसितो जीवस्तावन्निष्कलतां गतः ॥ १९॥

etasminvasate śīghramaviśrāntaṃ mahākhagaḥ |

yāvanniśvasito jīvastāvanniṣkalatāṃ gataḥ ‖ 19‖

नभस्थं निष्कलं ध्यात्वा मुच्यते भवबन्धनात्

अनाहतध्वनियुतं हंसं यो वेद हृद्गतम् ॥ २०॥

nabhasthaṃ niṣkalaṃ dhyātvā mucyate bhavabandhanāt

anāhatadhvaniyutaṃ haṃsaṃ yo veda hṛdgatam ‖ 20‖

Exposition of the cause of bondage and liberation

The JivA always recites the PraNavA with "I" and "He" consciousness. One should know this that "type of breadth going in and out, emanates from the region of navel is uncontaminated by connection with worldly concerns". JivA becomes one with

Brahman, through five-fold PrANAyAmA (i.e., PrANAyAmA, PratyAhArA, DhAraNa, DhyANA and SamAdhi) and engages itself in the heart with four-fold aspects of Vishva, Taijasa, PragnjA, and Turiya, and engages itself in the investigation of bondage, liberation, and their effects. As long as, Atman does not attain the knowledge, it restlessly wanders in and out, and once Atma Gjana is attained, the outgoing breadth carries with it, (JivA's internal organ stops functioning) the JivA attain state of cessation of diverse aspects and attains liberation by meditating upon the Brahman in the heart of PratygAtmA. (one's self Atma)

स्वप्रकाशचिदानन्दं स हंस इति गीयते ।
रेचकं पूरकं मुक्त्वा कुम्भकेन स्थितः सुधीः ॥ २१॥

svaprakāśacidānandaṃ sa haṃsa iti gīyate |
recakaṃ pūrakaṃ muktvā kumbhakena sthitaḥ sudhīḥ ॥ 21॥

नाभिकन्दे समौ कृत्वा प्राणापानौ समाहितः ।
मस्तकस्थामृतास्वादं पीत्वा ध्यानेन सादरम् ॥ २२॥

nābhikande samau kṛtvā prāṇāpānau samāhitaḥ |
mastakasthāmṛtāsvādaṃ pītvā dhyānena sādaram ॥ 22॥

दीपाकारं महादेवं ज्वलन्तं नाभिमध्यमे ।
अभिषिच्यामृतेनैव हंस हंसेति यो जपेत् ॥ २३॥

dīpākāraṃ mahādevaṃ jvalantaṃ nābhimadhyame |
abhiṣicyāmṛtenaiva haṃsa haṃseti yo japet ॥ 23॥

जरामरणरोगादि न तस्य भुवि विद्यते ।
एवं दिने दिने कुर्यादणिमादिविभूतये ॥ २४॥

jarāmaraṇarogādi na tasya bhuvi vidyate |

evaṃ dine dine kuryādaṇimādivibhūtaye || 24 ||

ईश्वरत्वमवाप्नोति सदाभ्यासरतः पुमान् ।

बहवो नैकमार्गेण प्राप्ता नित्यत्वमागताः || २५ ||

īśvaratvamavāpnoti sadābhyāsarataḥ pumān |

bahavo naikamārgeṇa prāptā nityatvamāgatāḥ || 25 ||

SLOKA 21-25

*Exposition of the cause of bondage and liberation
through hamsa vidya*

A yogi should after giving up Recaka, and Puraka must concentrate on Kumbaka, and bring PrANA and ApAnA vayus under equilibrium. Then "Hamsa" recitation brings him no death or disease in the world. All the side effects of getting siddhis on the way should never be misused. Then One attains oneness with Brahman. (Wielding marvellous Yogic Power) If Hamsa Vidya stops there is no means for attaining state of perpetual existence. Hamsa Vidya is the fifteenth among 108 Upanishads, and forms part of Sukla Yajur Veda. This also deals with esoteric nature of the Hamsavidya leading to Brahma Vidya.

This is formed in the manner of Question by Gautama Muni to Santkumara:

Gautama asks, "By what means is produced the awakening in the lore of Brahman?

Sanatkumara answers:

Hamsa Vidya is explained here by Sanatkumara; but he cautions that one has to learn it through a Guru and should not be communicated to those who do not believe in Brahmam. The detailed elaboration of the aspect of the Hamsa, bestows the fruit resulting from liberation. This denies enjoyment of everything except the Atma. The state of aloneness.

Hamsa Vidya Concept: Hamsa stands pervading the bodies of all beings from PrajApati the catur mukha Brahma down to a blade of grass, in the form of innermost JivA, and the transcendent Brahman-IshwarA) Having known that form, the knower does not attain the delusion relating to the existence of anything except Brahman. Yoga clearly explains the way to attain the knowledge of Hamsa.

Explanation of Hamsa MantrA (Author's note)

Hamsa is the rsi. (The seer of the mantra) Avyakta gayatri is the Chandas, Paramahamsa (Brahman is the deity) Ham is the Bija (Seed) Sah is the power(shakti) Soham is the Kilaka. In having the direct sight of the Hamsatman is the application (Viniyoga) Ham-sam is the Sixfold Anganyasa.

Now -Meditation (DhyAnA): I make salutations to the Hamsa i.e., who is the form of ParamAtmA, on whom the seekers and knowers of Brahman, meditate who takes his stand of the incoming and out going breadth, and with many other KalyANa GuNAs, takes His stand on the midst of mortals. Then the worship of the five elements, with their Bija letters Lam etc., So, Ham (I am He) is the Mantra. Exhale, inhale and reversal of the same alone constitute the Prayer. The uttering of the Prayer, as computed at the six centres of energy (by the presiding deities thereof) in the course of one day and night is 21600 times (in the form of So-Ham through expiration and inspiration) it goes on to explain the details which could be well read in YogA texts.

हंसविद्यामृते लोके नास्ति नित्यत्वसाधनम् ।

यो ददाति महाविद्यां हंसाख्यां पारमेश्वरीम् ॥ २६॥

haṃsavidyāmṛte loke nāsti nityatvasādhanam |

yo dadāti mahāvidyāṃ haṃsākhyāṃ pārameśvarīm || 26 ||

तस्य दास्यं सदा कुर्यात्प्रज्ञया परया सह ।

शुभं वाऽशुभमन्यद्वा यदुक्तं गुरुणा भुवि ॥ २७॥

tasya dāsyaṃ sadā kuryātprajñayā parayā saha |

śubhaṃ vā'śubhamanyadvā yaduktaṃ guruṇā bhuvi || 27 ||

तत्कुर्यादविचारेण शिष्यः सन्तोषसंयुतः ।
हंसविद्यामिमां लब्ध्वा गुरुशुश्रूषया नरः ॥ २८॥

tatkuryādavicāreṇa śiṣyaḥ santoṣasaṃyutaḥ ।
haṃsavidyāmimāṃ labdhvā guruśuśrūṣayā naraḥ ॥ 28॥

आत्मानमात्मना साक्षाद्ब्रह्म बुद्ध्वा सुनिश्चलम् ।
देहजात्यादिसम्बन्धान्वर्णाश्रमसमन्वितान् ॥ २९॥

ātmānamātmanā sākṣādbrahma buddhvā suniścalam ।
dehajātyādisambandhānvarṇāśramasamanvitān ॥ 29॥

वेदशास्त्राणि चान्यानि पदपांसुमिव त्यजेत् ।
गुरुभक्तिं सदा कुर्याच्छ्रेयसे भूयसे नरः ॥ ३०॥

vedaśāstrāṇi cānyāni padapāṃsumiva tyajet ।
gurubhaktiṃ sadā kuryācchreyase bhūyase naraḥ ॥ 30॥

गुरुरेव हरिः साक्षान्नान्य इत्यब्रवीच्छ्रुतिः ॥ ३१॥

gurureva hariḥ sākṣānnānya ityabravīcchṛtiḥ ॥ 31॥

Rule of devotion to the guru of hamsavidya

Sruti states the importance Hamsa Vidya, Guru Thus:

He who wants to know the Highest Hamsa vidya always to service Him, with superior wisdom. Whatever in this world, productive of happiness, misery, or otherwise is the mandate of the Guru, that the disciple should carry out with utmost, pleasure, without any scruple whatsoever. Once this highest knowledge is obtained through the Guru, that Atman is no other than non-fickle Brahman, that person should renounce the SamsArA along with VAsanAs, and treat Guru with extreme reverence. Guru alone is Hari incarnate says Sruti.

श्रुत्या यदुक्तं परमार्थमेव

तत्संशयो नात्र ततः समस्तम् ।

श्रुत्या विरोधे न भवेत्प्रमाणं

भवेदनर्थाय विना प्रमाणम् ॥ ३२ ॥

śrutyā yaduktaṃ paramārthameva

tatsaṃśayo nātra tataḥ samastam |

śrutyā virodhe na bhavetpramāṇam

bhavedanarthāya vinā pramāṇam || 32||

देहस्थः सकलो ज्ञेयो निष्कलो देहवर्जितः ।

आप्तोपदेशगम्योऽसौ सर्वतः समवस्थितः ॥ ३३ ॥

dehasthaḥ sakalo jñeyo niṣkalo dehavarjitaḥ |

āptopadeśagamyo'sau sarvataḥ samavasthitaḥ || 33||

हंसहंसेति यो ब्रूयाद्धंसो ब्रह्मा हरिः शिवः ।

गुरुवक्त्रात्तु लभ्येत प्रत्यक्षं सर्वतोमुखम् ॥ ३४ ॥

haṃsahaṃseti yo brūyāddhaṃso brahmā hariḥ śivaḥ |

guruvaktrāttu labhyeta pratyakṣaṃ sarvatomukham || 34||

तिलेषु च यथा तैलं पुष्पे गन्ध इवाश्रितः ।
पुरुषस्य शरीरेऽस्मिन्स बाह्याभ्यन्तरे तथा ॥ ३५ ॥

tileṣu ca yathā tailaṁ puṣpe gandha ivāśritaḥ |
puruṣasya śarīre'sminsa bāhyābhyantare tathā ॥ 35॥

<hr>

SLOKA 32-35

*The attainability of the brahman solelythrough vedas
and guru*

<hr>

He (Brahman) stands, pervading the exterior and interior of all beings that is created. And one should obtain this secret through the mouth of an experienced Guru. What is related by VedA is the supreme end of the existence. There is no doubt about it. Therefrom flow all things. Should there be divergence from VedA that will not afford sanction. Anything without sanction will contribute towards utter ruin Brahman is attainable only through sound precept. Why then Brahman is said to be in all direction. Those who have had MantrOpadesam through a Guru, is directly cognisized, and faces in all directions.

उल्काहस्तो यथालोके द्रव्यमालोक्य तां त्यजेत् ।
ज्ञानेन ज्ञेयमालोक्य पश्चाज्ज्ञानं परित्यजेत् ॥ ३६ ॥

ulkāhasto yathāloke dravyamālokya tāṁ tyajet |
jñānena jñeyamālokya paścājjñānaṁ parityajet ॥ 36॥

पुष्पवत्सकलं विद्याद्गन्धस्तस्य तु निष्कलः ।
वृक्षस्तु सकलं विद्याच्छाया तस्य तु निष्कला ॥ ३७ ॥

puṣpavatsakalaṁ vidyādgandhastasya tu niṣkalaḥ |
vṛkṣastu sakalaṁ vidyācchāyā tasya tu niṣkalā ॥ 37॥

निष्कलः सकलो भावः सर्वत्रैव व्यवस्थितः ।
उपायः सकलस्तद्वदुपेयश्चैव निष्कलः ॥ ३८॥

niṣkalaḥ sakalo bhāvaḥ sarvatraiva vyavasthitaḥ |
upāyaḥ sakalastadvadupeyaścaiva niṣkalaḥ ॥ 38॥

सकले सकलो भावो निष्कले निष्कलस्तथा ।
एकमात्रो द्विमात्रश्च त्रिमात्रश्चैव भेदतः ॥ ३९॥

sakale sakalo bhāvo niṣkale niṣkalastathā |
ekamātro dvimātraśca trimātraścaiva bhedataḥ ॥ 39॥

अर्धमात्र परा ज्ञेया तत ऊर्ध्वं परात्परम् ।
पञ्चधा पञ्चदैवत्यं सकलं परिपठ्यते ॥ ४०॥

ardhamātra parā jñeyā tata ūrdhvaṃ parātparam |
pañcadhā pañcadaivatyaṃ sakalam paripaṭhyate ॥ 40॥

ब्रह्मणो हृदयस्थानं कण्ठे विष्णुः समाश्रितः ।
तालुमध्ये स्थितो रुद्रो ललाटस्थो महेश्वरः ॥ ४१॥

brahmaṇo hṛdayasthānaṃ kaṇṭhe viṣṇuḥ samāśritaḥ |
tālumadhye sthito rudro lalāṭastho maheśvaraḥ ॥ 41॥

नासाग्रे अच्युतं विद्यात्तस्यान्ते तु परं पदम् ।
परत्वात्तु परं नास्तीत्येवं शास्त्रस्य निर्णयः ॥ ४२ ॥

nāsāgre acyutaṃ vidyāttasyānte tu paraṃ padam |

paratvāttu paraṃ nāstītyevaṃ śāstrasya nirṇayaḥ ॥ 42 ॥

देहातीतं तु तं विद्यान्नासाग्रे द्वादशाङ्गुलम् ।
तदन्तं तं विजानीयात्तत्रस्थो व्यापयेत्प्रभुः ॥ ४३ ॥

dehātītaṃ tu taṃ vidyānnāsāgre dvādaśāṅgulam |

tadantaṃ taṃ vijānīyāttatrastho vyāpayetprabhuḥ ॥ 43 ॥

SLOKA 36-43

Discimination between atman and paramatman

One should realise through a Guru that Atman is finite and Brahman is infinite. In the seat of the Heart is Brahman. The seat one should know as DehAatita (which transcends the body) where in seated the innermost Atman (The Brahman) twelve inches from the tip of the nose. Here Brahman is seated and pervades everywhere

मनोऽप्यन्यत्र निक्षिप्तं चक्षुरन्यत्र पातितम् ।
तथापि योगिनां योगो ह्यविच्छिन्नः प्रवर्तते ॥ ४४ ॥

mano'pyanyatra nikṣiptaṃ cakṣuranyatra pātitam |

tathāpi yogināṃ yogo hyavicchinnaḥ pravartate ॥ 44 ॥

एतत्तु परमं गुह्यमेतत्तु परमं शुभम् ।
नातः परतरं किञ्चिन्नातः परतरं शुभम् ॥ ४५ ॥

etattu paramaṃ guhyametattu paramaṃ śubham |

nātaḥ parataraṃ kiñcinnataḥ parataraṃ śubham || 45 ||

शुद्धज्ञानामृतं प्राप्य परमाक्षरनिर्णयम् ।

गुह्याद्गुह्यतमं गोप्यं ग्रहणीयं प्रयत्नतः ॥ ४६॥

śuddhajñānāmṛtaṃ prāpya paramākṣaranirṇayam |

guhyādguhyatamaṃ gopyaṃ grahaṇīyaṃ prayatnataḥ || 46 ||

नापुत्राय प्रदातव्यं नाशिष्याय कदाचन ।

गुरुदेवाय भक्ताय नित्यं भक्तिपराय च ॥ ४७॥

nāputrāya pradātavyaṃ nāśiṣyāya kadācana |

gurudevāya bhaktāya nityaṃ bhaktiparāya ca || 47 ||

प्रदातव्यमिदं शास्त्रं नेतरेभ्यः प्रदापयेत् ।

दातास्य नरकं याति सिद्ध्यते न कदाचन ॥ ४८॥

pradātavyamidaṃ śāstraṃ netarebhyaḥ pradāpayet |

dātāsya narakaṃ yāti siddhyate na kadācana || 48 ||

This yoga to be bestowed

The fruit of YogA worthy of being kept as a profound secret and is conducive of doing great good. This secret learned through YogA by a devoted shishyA who looks upon his Guru as God incarnate, and is ever ready to show his devotion to the Guru. One should never bestow this to others.

गृहस्थो ब्रह्मचारी च वानप्रस्थश्च भिक्षुकः ।
यत्र तत्र स्थितो ज्ञानी परमाक्षरवित्सदा ॥ ४९॥

gṛhastho brahmacārī ca vānaprasthaśca bhikṣukaḥ ।
yatra tatra sthito jñānī paramākṣaravitsadā ॥ 49॥

विषयी विषयासक्तो याति देहान्तरे शुभम् ।
ज्ञानादेवास्य शास्त्रस्य सर्वावस्थोऽपि मानवः ॥ ५०॥

viṣayī viṣayāsakto yāti dehāntare śubham ।
jñānādevāsya śāstrasya sarvāvastho'pi mānavaḥ ॥ 50॥

---

*This highest knowledge alone does not give someone
vice and virtue*

Only by acquiring this knowledge alone through a Guru does not give happiness to someone entering other body.

ब्रह्महत्याश्वमेधाद्यैः पुण्यपापैर्न लिप्यते ।
चोदको बोधकश्चैव मोक्षदश्च परः स्मृतः ॥ ५१॥

brahmahatyāśvamedhādyaiḥ puṇyapāpairna lipyate ।
codako bodhakaścaiva mokṣadaśca paraḥ smṛtaḥ ॥ 51॥

इत्येषं त्रिविधो ज्ञेय आचार्यस्तु महीतले ।
चोदको दर्शयेन्मार्गं बोधकः स्थानमाचरेत् ॥ ५२॥

ityeṣaṃ trividho jñeya ācāryastu mahītale |

codako darśayenmārgaṃ bodhakaḥ sthānamācaret || 52 ||

Who is real perceptor (three things he must do)

Supreme Guru should do following to his ShishyA.

The prompter, the awakener, and the bestower of Liberation

मोक्षदस्तु परं तत्त्वं यज्ज्ञात्वा परमश्नुते ।
प्रत्यक्षयजनं देहे संक्षेपाच्छृणु गौतम ॥ ५३ ॥

mokṣadastu paraṃ tattvam yajjñātvā paramaśnute |

pratyakṣayajanaṃ dehe samkṣepācchṛṇu gautama || 53 ||

तेनेष्ट्वा स नरो याति शाश्वतं पदमव्ययम् ।
स्वयमेव तु सम्पश्येद्देहे बिन्दुं च निष्कलम् ॥ ५४ ॥

teneṣṭvā sa naro yāti śāśvataṃ padamavyayam |

svayameva tu sampaśyeddehe bindum ca niṣkalam || 54 ||

अयने द्वे च विषुवे सदा पश्यति मार्गवित् ।
कृत्वायामं पुरा वत्स रेचपूरककुम्भकान् ॥ ५५ ॥

ayane dve ca viṣuve sadā paśyati mārgavit |

kṛtvāyāmam purā vatsa recapūrakakumbhakān || 55 ||

पूर्वं चोभयमुच्चार्य अर्चयेतु यथाक्रमम् ।
नमस्कारेण योगेन मुद्रयारभ्य चार्चयेत् ॥ ५६॥

pūrvaṃ cobhayamuccārya arcayettu yathākramam |

namaskāreṇa yogena mudrayārabhya cārcayet ॥ 56 ॥

SLOKA 53-56

The performance of sacrifice in the immediate presence
of brahman by applying pranava hamsa

Briefly, the sacrifice to be performed in the immediate presence of Brahman, is in the Body itself. Whence performed this, the sacrifice reaches the eternal and undecaying state. This sacrifice is performed thus:Perform Recaka, Puraka and Kumbaka for one Yama (three hours) every day, and then if recited the Japa, the PraNavA and Hamsa MantrA, along with application of his mind to their fullest in the proper order and reverently worship the Brahman, commencing with prostration and assuming with Chin MudrA and uttering the word He am I, being lost in communion with it. The eclipse of the Sun is thought of as direct sacrifice.

सूर्यस्य ग्रहणं वत्स प्रत्यक्षयजनं स्मृतम् ।
ज्ञानात्सायुज्यमेवोक्तं तोये तोयं यथा तथा ॥ ५७॥

sūryasya grahaṇaṃ vatsa pratyakṣayajanaṃ smṛtam |

jñānātsāyujyamevoktaṃ toye toyaṃ yathā tathā ॥ 57 ॥

एते गुणाः प्रवर्तन्ते योगाभ्यासकृतश्रमैः ।
तस्माद्योगं समादाय सर्वदुःखबहिष्कृतः ॥ ५८॥

ete guṇāḥ pravartante yogābhyāsakṛtaśramaiḥ |

tasmādyogaṃ samādāya sarvaduḥkhabahiṣkṛtaḥ ॥ 58 ॥

योगध्यानं सदा कृत्वा ज्ञानं तन्मयतां व्रजेत् ।

ज्ञानात्स्वरूपं परमं हंसमन्त्रं समुच्चरेत् ॥ ५९॥

yogadhyānaṃ sadā kṛtvā jñānaṃ tanmayatāṃ vrajet |

jñānātsvarūpaṃ paramaṃ haṃsamantraṃ samuccaret || 59||

SLOKA 57-59

*The attainment of becoming one with the brahman
through the knowledge obtained from hamsa yoga*

It has been said that from knowledge is attained, oneness of Atman and Brahman. For this practice, the Yogin become s one with Brahman, and the Yogin is divorced from all sufferings, and pain. Therefore, one should always practice Yogic Meditation and attain wisdom, and with this wisdom merge with Brahman.

प्राणिनां देहमध्ये तु स्थितो हंसः सदाच्युतः ।

हंस एव परं सत्यं हंस एव तु शक्तिकम् ॥ ६०॥

prāṇināṃ dehamadhye tu sthito haṃsaḥ sadācyutaḥ |

haṃsa eva paraṃ satyaṃ haṃsa eva tu śaktikam || 60||

हंस एव परं वाक्यं हंस एव तु वादिकम् ।

हंस एव परो रुद्रो हंस एव परात्परम् ॥ ६१॥

haṃsa eva paraṃ vākyaṃ haṃsa eva tu vādikam |

haṃsa eva paro rudro haṃsa eva parātparam || 61||

सर्वदेवस्य मध्यस्थो हंस एव महेश्वरः ।

पृथिव्यादिशिवान्तं तु अकाराद्याश्च वर्णकाः ॥ ६२॥

sarvadevasya madhyastho haṃsa eva maheśvaraḥ ।

pṛthivyādiśivāntaṃ tu akārādyāśca varṇakāḥ ॥ 62॥

Hamsa the Brahman has His abode in the Heart in the middle of the body of all beings along with all His KalyaNa guNA. He alone is attached to fifty-one letters (AksharA) commencing from **"अ"** and ending with Koota" (Ksha) **"क्ष"**

कूटान्ता हंस एव स्यान्मातृकेति व्यवस्थिताः ।
मातृकारहितं मन्त्रमादिशन्ते न कुत्रचित् ॥ ६३ ॥

kūṭāntā haṃsa eva syānmātṛketi vyavasthitāḥ ।
mātṛkārahitaṃ mantramādiśante na kutracit ॥ 63॥

हंसज्योतिरनूपम्यं मध्ये देवं व्यवस्थितम् ।
दक्षिणामुखमाश्रित्य ज्ञानमुद्रां प्रकल्पयेत् ॥ ६४॥

haṃsajyotiranūpamyaṃ madhye devaṃ vyavasthitam ।
dakṣiṇāmukhamāśritya jñānamudrāṃ prakalpayet ॥ 64॥

सदा समाधिं कुर्वीत हंसमन्त्रमनुस्मरन् ।
निर्मलस्फटिकाकारं दिव्यरूपमनुत्तमम् ॥ ६५॥

sadā samādhiṃ kurvīta haṃsamantramanusmaran ।
nirmalasphaṭikākāraṃ divyarūpamanuttamam ॥ 65॥

Practice of samadhi preced by the hamsa mantra

Nowhere, do people recognise a Mantra made up of sounds which have no counterparts in the alphabet. One should seek protection at the hands of the Hamsa radiance well placed with GjAna MudrA **(ज्ञानमुद्रा)** posture. He should be always be concentrated and always reciting the Hamsa -mantra.

मध्यदेशे परं हंसं ज्ञानमुद्रात्मरूपकम् ।

प्राणोऽपानः समानश्चोदानव्यानौ च वायवः ॥ ६६॥

madhyadeśe param haṃsam jñānamudrātmarūpakam |

prāṇo'pānaḥ samānaścodānavyānau ca vāyavaḥ ॥ 66॥

पञ्चकर्मेन्द्रियैरुक्ताः क्रियाशक्तिबलोद्यताः ।

नागः कूर्मश्च कृकरो देवदत्तो धनञ्जयः ॥ ६७॥

pañcakarmendriyairuktāḥ kriyāśaktibalodyatāḥ |

nāgaḥ kūrmaśca kṛkaro devadatto dhanañjayaḥ ॥ 67॥

पञ्चज्ञानेन्द्रियैर्युक्ता ज्ञानशक्तिबलोद्यताः ।

पावकः शक्तिमध्ये तु नाभिचक्रे रविः स्थितः ॥ ६८॥

pañcajñānendriyairyuktā jñānaśaktibalodyatāḥ |

pāvakaḥ śaktimadhye tu nābhicakre raviḥ sthitaḥ ॥ 68॥

Exposition of posture assumed by hamsa

Pure Yogic explanation:

The five vital airs Prana, Apana, Samana, Udana and Vyana, in conjunction with five inner senses are enthused by the strength of Kriya shakti (Power of doing deeds) the five vital airs, Naga, Kurma, krkara, Devadatta, and Dhananjaya in conjunction with inner senses of perception are enthused by the strength of Gjana shakti (the power of knowledge) Hamsa alone stands in the fire midway between two shaktis.

बन्धमुद्रा कृता येन नासाग्रे तु स्वलोचने ।
अकारेवह्निरित्याहुरुकारे हृदि संस्थितः ॥ ६९॥

bandhamudrā kṛtā yena nāsāgre tu svalocane |

akārevahnirityāhurukāre hṛdi saṃsthitaḥ ॥ 69॥

मकारे च भ्रुवोर्मध्ये प्राणशक्त्या प्रबोधयेत् ।
ब्रह्मग्रन्थिरकारे च विष्णुग्रन्थिर्हृदि स्थितः ॥ ७०॥

makāre ca bhruvormadhye prāṇaśaktyā prabodhayet |

brahmagranthirakāre ca viṣṇugranthirhṛdi sthitaḥ ॥ 70॥

रुद्रग्रन्थिर्भ्रुवोर्मध्ये भिद्यतेऽक्षरवायुना ।
अकारे संस्थितो ब्रह्मा उकारे विष्णुरास्थितः ॥ ७१॥

rudragranthirbhruvormadhye bhidyate'kṣaravāyunā |

akāre saṃsthito brahmā ukāre viṣṇurāsthitaḥ ॥ 71॥

मकारे संस्थितो रुद्रस्ततोऽस्यान्तः परात्परः ।
कण्ठं सङ्कुच्य नाड्यादौ स्तम्भिते येन शक्तितः ॥ ७२ ॥

makāre saṃsthito rudrastato'syāntaḥ parātparaḥ |
kaṇṭhaṃ saṅkucya nāḍyādau stambhite yena śaktitaḥ ‖ 72 ‖

रसना पीड्यमानेयं षोडशी वोर्ध्वगामिनि ।
त्रिकूटं त्रिविधा चैव गोलाखं निखरं तथा ॥ ७३ ॥

rasanā pīḍyamāneyaṃ ṣoḍaśī vordhvagāmini |
trikūṭaṃ trividhā caiva golākhaṃ nikharaṃ tathā ‖ 73 ‖

त्रिशङ्खवज्रमोङ्कारमूर्ध्वनालं भ्रुवोर्मुखम् ।
कुण्डलीं चालयन्प्राणान्भेदयन्शशिमण्डलम् ॥ ७४ ॥

triśaṅkhavajramoṅkāramūrdhvanālaṃ bhruvormukham |
kuṇḍalīṃ cālayanprāṇānbhedayanśaśimaṇḍalam ‖ 74 ‖

साधयन्वज्रकुम्भानि नवद्वाराणि बन्धयेत् ।
सुमनःपवनारूढः सरागो निर्गुणस्तथा ॥ ७५ ॥

sādhayanvajrakumbhāni navadvārāṇi bandhayet |
sumanaḥpavanārūḍhaḥ sarāgo nirguṇastathā ‖ 75 ‖

ब्रह्मस्थाने तु नादः स्याच्छाकिन्यामृतवर्षिणी ।
षट्चक्रमण्डलोद्धारं ज्ञानदीपं प्रकाशयेत् ॥ ७६ ॥

brahmasthāne tu nādaḥ syācchākinyāmṛtavarṣiṇī |
ṣaṭcakramaṇḍaloddhāraṃ jñānadīpaṃ prakāśayet ‖ 76 ‖

सर्वभूतस्थितं देवं सर्वेशं नित्यमर्चयेत् ।
आत्मरूपं तमालोक्य ज्ञानरूपं निरामयम् ॥ ७७॥

sarvabhūtasthitaṃ devaṃ sarveśaṃ nityamarcayet |
ātmarūpaṃ tamālokya jñānarūpaṃ nirāmayam || 77 ||

दृश्यन्तं दिव्यरूपेण सर्वव्यापी निरञ्जनः ।
हंस हंस वदेद्वाक्यं प्राणिनां देहमाश्रितः ।
सप्राणापानयोर्ग्रन्थिरजपेत्यभिधीयते ॥ ७८॥

dṛśyantaṃ divyarūpeṇa sarvavyāpī nirañjanaḥ |
haṃsa haṃsa vadedvākyaṃ prāṇināṃ dehamāśritaḥ |
saprāṇāpānayorgranthirajapetyabhidhīyate || 78 ||

सहस्रमेकं द्वयुतं षट्शतं चैव सर्वदा ।
उच्चरन्पठितो हंसः सोऽहमित्यभिधीयते ॥ ७९॥

sahasramekaṃ dvayutaṃ ṣaṭśataṃ caiva sarvadā |
uccaranpaṭhito haṃsaḥ so'hamityabhidhīyate || 79 ||

पूर्वभागे ह्यधोलिङ्गं शिखिन्यां चैव पश्चिमम् ।
ज्योतिर्लिङ्गं भ्रुवोर्मध्ये नित्यं ध्यायेत्सदा यतिः ॥ ८०॥

pūrvabhāge hyadholiṅgaṃ śikhinyāṃ caiva paścimam |
jyotirliṅgaṃ bhruvormadhye nityaṃ dhyāyetsadā yatiḥ || 80 ||

The mode of practicing the hamsa yoga

Utterance of Pranava is what transcends knots in the Nadis and supreme being the Brahman. Then Kundalini Yoga and moving that shakti up is described. In the seat of Brahman, there will become manifest the nada.(sound) Knower of Brahman should then worship Brahman in the form of knowledge.

अच्युतोऽहमचिन्त्योऽहमतर्क्योऽहमजोऽस्म्यहम् ।

अप्राणोऽहमकायोऽहमनङ्गोऽस्म्यभयोऽस्म्यहम् ॥ ८१॥

acyuto'hamacintyo'hamatarkyo'hamajo'smyaham |

aprāṇo'hamakāyo'hamanaṅgo'smyabhayo'smyaham || 81 ||

अशब्दोऽहमरूपोऽहमस्पर्शोऽस्म्यहमद्वयः ।

अरसोऽहमगन्धोऽहमनादिरमृतोऽस्म्यहम् ॥ ८२॥

aśabdo'hamarūpo'hamasparśo'smyahamadvayaḥ |

araso'hamagandho'hamanādiramṛto'smyaham || 82 ||

अक्षयोऽहमलिङ्गोऽहमजरोऽस्म्यकलोऽस्म्यहम् ।

अप्राणोऽहममूकोऽहमचिन्त्योऽस्म्यकृतोऽस्म्यहम् ॥ ८३॥

akṣayo'hamaliṅgo'hamajaro'smyakalo'smyaham |

aprāṇo'hamamūko'hamacintyo'smyakṛto'smyaham || 83 ||

अन्तर्याम्यहमग्राह्योऽनिर्देश्योऽहमलक्षणः ।

अगोत्रोऽहमगात्रोऽहमचक्षुष्कोऽस्म्यवागहम् ॥ ८४॥

antaryāmyahamagrāhyo'nirdeśyo'hamalakṣaṇaḥ |
agotro'hamagātro'hamacakṣuṣko'smyavāgaham || 84||

अदृश्योऽहमवर्णोऽहमखण्डोऽस्म्यहमद्भुतः ।
अश्रुतोऽहमदृष्टोऽहमन्वेष्टव्योऽमरोऽस्म्यहम् ॥ ८५॥

adṛśyo'hamavarṇo'hamakhaṇḍo'smyahamadbhutaḥ |
aśruto'hamadṛṣṭo'hamanveṣṭavyo'maro'smyaham || 85||

अवायुरप्यनाकाशोऽतेजस्कोऽव्यभिचार्यहम् ।
अमतोऽहमजातोऽहमतिसूक्ष्मोऽविकार्यहम् ॥ ८६॥

avāyurapyanākāśo'tejasko'vyabhicāryaham |
amato'hamajāto'hamatisūkṣmo'vikāryaham || 86||

अरजस्कोऽतमस्कोऽहमसत्त्वोस्म्यगुणोऽस्म्यहम् ।
अमायोऽनुभवात्माहमनन्योऽविषयोऽस्म्यहम् ॥ ८७॥

arajasko'tamasko'hamasattvosmyaguṇo'smyaham |
amāyo'nubhavātmāhamananyo'viṣayo'smyaham || 87||

अद्वैतोऽहमपूर्णोऽहमबाह्योऽहमनन्तरः ।
अश्रोतोऽहमदीर्घोऽहमव्यक्तोऽहमनामयः ॥ ८८॥

advaito'hamapūrṇo'hamabāhyo'hamanantaraḥ |
aśroto'hamadīrgho'hamavyakto'hamanāmayaḥ || 88||

अद्वयानन्दविज्ञानघनोऽस्म्यहमविक्रियः ।
अनिच्छोऽहमलेपोऽहमकर्तास्म्यहमद्वयः ॥ ८९॥

advayānandavijñānaghano'smyahamavikriyaḥ |
aniccho'hamalepo'hamakartāsmyahamadvayaḥ || 89||

अविद्याकार्यहीनोऽहमवाग्रसनगोचरः |
अनल्पोऽहमशोकोऽहमविकल्पोऽस्म्यविज्वलन् || ९०||

avidyākāryahīno'hamavāgrasanagocaraḥ |
analpo'hamaśoko'hamavikalpo'smyavijvalan || 90||

आदिमध्यान्तहीनोऽहमाकाशसदृशोऽस्म्यहम् |
आत्मचैतन्यरूपोऽहमहमानन्दचिद्धनः || ९१||

ādimadhyāntahīno'hamākāśasadṛśo'smyaham |
ātmacaitanyarūpo'hamahamānandacidghanaḥ || 91||

आनन्दामृतरूपोऽहमात्मसंस्थोहमन्तरः |
आत्मकामोहमाकाशात्परमात्मेश्वरोस्म्यहम् || ९२||

ānandāmṛtarūpo'hamātmasaṃsthohamantaraḥ |
ātmakāmohamākāśātparamātmeśvarosmyaham || 92||

ईशानोस्म्यहमीड्योऽहमहमुत्तमपूरुषः |
उत्कृष्टोऽहमुपद्रष्टा अहमुत्तरतोऽस्म्यहम् || ९३||

īśānosmyahamīḍyo'hamahamuttamapūruṣaḥ |
utkṛṣṭo'hamupadraṣṭā ahamuttarato'smyaham || 93||

केवलोऽहं कविः कर्माध्यक्षोऽहं करणाधिपः |
गुहाशयोऽहं गोसाहं चक्षुष्चक्षुरस्म्यहम् || ९४||

kevalo'haṃ kaviḥ karmādhyakṣo'haṃ karaṇādhipaḥ |
guhāśayo'haṃ goptāhaṃ cakṣuṣaścakṣurasmyaham || 94||

चिदानन्दोऽस्म्यहं चेता चिद्घनश्चिन्मयोऽस्म्यहम् |
ज्योतिर्मयोऽस्म्यहं ज्यायाञ्ज्योतिषां ज्योतिरस्म्यहम् || ९५ ||

cidānando'smyahaṃ cetā cidghanaścinmayo'smyaham |
jyotirmayo'smyahaṃ jyāyāñjyotiṣāṃ jyotirasmyaham || 95||

तमसः साक्ष्यहं तुर्यतुर्योऽहं तमसः परः |
दिव्यो देवोऽस्मि दुर्दर्शो दृष्टाध्यायो ध्रुवोऽस्म्यहम् || ९६ ||

tamasaḥ sākṣyahaṃ turyaturyo'haṃ tamasaḥ paraḥ |
divyo devo'smi durdarśo dṛṣṭādhyāyo dhruvo'smyaham || 96||

नित्योऽहं निरवद्योऽहं निष्क्रियोऽस्मि निरञ्जनः |
निर्मलो निर्विकल्पोऽहं निराख्यातोऽस्मि निश्चलः || ९७ ||

nityo'haṃ niravadyo'haṃ niṣkriyo'smi nirañjanaḥ |
nirmalo nirvikalpo'haṃ nirākhyāto'smi niścalaḥ || 97||

निर्विकारो नित्यपूतो निर्गुणो निःस्पृहोऽस्म्यहम् |
निरिन्द्रियो नियन्ताहं निरपेक्षोऽस्मि निष्कलः || ९८ ||

nirvikāro nityapūto nirguṇo niḥspṛho'smyaham |
nirindriyo niyantāhaṃ nirapekṣo'smi niṣkalaḥ || 98||

पुरुषः परमात्माहं पुराणः परमोऽस्म्यहम् |
परावरोऽस्म्यहं प्राज्ञः प्रपञ्चोपशमोऽस्म्यहम् || ९९ ||

puruṣaḥ paramātmāhaṃ purāṇaḥ paramo'smyaham |
parāvaro'smyahaṃ prājñaḥ prapañcopaśamo'smyaham || 99 ||

परामृतोऽस्म्यहं पूर्णः प्रभुरस्मि पुरातनः |
पूर्णानन्दैकबोधोऽहं प्रत्यगेकरसोऽस्म्यहम् || १०० ||

parāmṛto'smyahaṃ pūrṇaḥ prabhurasmi purātanaḥ |
pūrṇānandaikabodho'haṃ pratyagekaraso'smyaham || 100 ||

प्रज्ञातोऽहं प्रशान्तोऽहं प्रकाशः परमेश्वरः |
एकदा चिन्त्यमानोऽहं द्वैताद्वैतविलक्षणः || १०१ ||

prajñāto'haṃ praśānto'haṃ prakāśaḥ parameśvaraḥ |
ekadā cintyamāno'haṃ dvaitādvaitavilakṣaṇaḥ || 101 ||

बुद्धोऽहं भूतपालोऽहं भारूपो भगवानहम् |
महाज्ञेयो महानस्मि महाज्ञेयो महेश्वरः || १०२ ||

buddho'haṃ bhūtapālo'haṃ bhārūpo bhagavānaham |
mahājñeyo mahānasmi mahājñeyo maheśvaraḥ || 102 ||

विमुक्तोऽहं विभुरहं वरेण्यो व्यापकोऽस्म्यहम् |
वैश्वानरो वासुदेवो विश्वतश्चक्षुरस्म्यहम् || १०३ ||

vimukto'haṃ vibhurahaṃ vareṇyo vyāpako'smyaham |
vaiśvānaro vāsudevo viśvataścakṣurasmyaham || 103 ||

विश्वाधिकोऽहं विशदो विष्णुर्विश्वकृदस्म्यहम् |
शुद्धोऽस्मि शुक्रः शान्तोऽस्मि शाश्वतोऽस्मि शिवोऽस्म्यहम् || १०४ ||

viśvādhiko'haṃ viśado viṣṇurviśvakṛdasmyaham |
śuddho'smi śukraḥ śānto'smi śāśvato'smi śivo'smyaham || 104||

सर्वभूतान्तरात्महमहमस्मि सनातनः ।
अहं सकृद्विभातोऽस्मि स्वे महिम्नि सदा स्थितः ॥ १०५ ॥

sarvabhūtāntarātmahamahamasmi sanātanaḥ |
ahaṃ sakṛdvibhāto'smi sve mahimni sadā sthitaḥ || 105 ||

सर्वान्तरः स्वयंज्योतिः सर्वाधिपतिरस्म्यहम् ।
सर्वभूताधिवासोऽहं सर्वव्यापी स्वराडहम् ॥ १०६ ॥

sarvāntaraḥ svayaṃjyotiḥ sarvādhipatirasmyaham |
sarvabhūtādhivāso'haṃ sarvavyāpī svarāḍaham || 106 ||

समस्तसाक्षी सर्वात्मा सर्वभूतगुहाशयः ।
सर्वेन्द्रियगुणाभासः सर्वेन्द्रियविवर्जितः ॥ १०७ ॥

samastasākṣī sarvātmā sarvabhūtaguhāśayaḥ |
sarvendriyaguṇābhāsaḥ sarvendriyavivarjitaḥ || 107 ||

स्थानत्रयव्यतीतोऽहं सर्वानुग्राहकोऽस्म्यहम् ।
सच्चिदानन्द पूर्णात्मा सर्वप्रेमास्पदोऽस्म्यहम् ॥ १०८ ॥

sthānatrayavyatīto'haṃ sarvānugrāhako'smyaham |
saccidānanda pūrṇātmā sarvapremāspado'smyaham || 108 ||

सच्चिदानन्दमात्रोऽहं स्वप्रकाशोऽस्मि चिद्घनः ।
सत्त्वस्वरूपसन्मात्रसिद्धसर्वात्मकोऽस्म्यहम् ॥ १०९ ॥

saccidānandamātro'haṃ svaprakāśo'smi cidghanaḥ |
sattvasvarūpasanmātrasiddhasarvātmako'smyaham || 109 ||

सर्वाधिष्ठानसन्मात्रः स्वात्मबन्धहरोऽस्म्यहम् ।
सर्वग्रासोऽस्म्यहं सर्वद्रष्टा सर्वानुभूरहम् ॥ ११० ॥

sarvādhiṣṭhānasanmātraḥ svātmabandhaharo'smyaham ǀ
sarvagrāso'smyahaṃ sarvadraṣṭā sarvānubhūraham ǁ 110 ǁ

---

*The real form of the atman to be contemplated upon by
the hamsa-yogin*

I am the manifestation of the senses and their Gunas, and devoid of all senses
I have my seat beyond the three states (waking, sleeping, and dreaming) I
bestow my favour on all. Then, it goes on to explain the eight Gunas of Atma
we saw in the conclusion, Apahatapapma ......

एवं यो वेद तत्त्वेन स वै पुरुष उच्यत इत्युपनिषत् ǁ

evaṃ yo veda tattvena sa vai puruṣa ucyata ityupaniṣat ǁ

ॐ सह नाववतु ǁ सह नौ भुनक्तु ǁ सह वीर्यं करवावहै ǁ

oṃ saha nāvavatu ǁ saha nau bhunaktu ǁ saha vīryaṃ karavāvahai ǁ

तेजस्विनावधीतमस्तु मा विद्विषावहै ǁ

tejasvināvadhītamastu mā vidviṣāvahai ǁ

ॐ शान्तिः शान्तिः शान्तिः ǁ

13. Conclusion

PratyagAtma and ParamAtmA-

The secret of Brahmavidyā is to reveal the real nature of the Ātmā, that is all-pervading, that is like ghee in the milk, that is the source of <u>Atmavidyā</u> and <u>Tapas</u> and to show that everything is in essence one. This is the English translation of the Brahma Upanishad (belonging to the Krishna-Yajurveda). (From Sri. Narayanaswamy's transliteration of Brahma Vidya from the book "Thirty Minor Upanishads" published in the Year 1914.

According to Vishishtadvaita philosophy Surrender (NyAsA) as stated is the best option for JivA for Liberation.

I will narrate here another Important AcharyA Sri.Alawandar's (Sri Ramanauja's Guru)Storaratna and what he says about NyAsA.

Sri Nathamuni and Sri Yamuna occupy a central position (*Natha-Yamuna madhyamam*) among the illustrious Acharyas, who reformed and revitalized the ancient system of thought and faith – *Vishitadvaita Siddantha*

Sri Ramanuja inherited that rich heritage; and enhanced it further. It was on the basis of the works of his Grand Acharya (*Pracharya**) *i. e.*, Sri Yamunacharya, that Sri Ramanuja, later, established, fortified and perfected the *Vishistadvaita Siddantha*. [*Sri Yāmunācārya was said to be the preceptor of Mahāpūrṇa who initiated Sri Rāmānuja.]

Stotra-ratna

Stotra-ratna and Chatus-sloki are hymns singing the glory and splendour of Lord Vishnu and Devi Lakshmi. They are the fervent outpouring of Sri Yamuna's intense devotion towards Vishnu and Lakshmi; and, his deep-rooted longing for communion with his favourite deity

The Stotra-Ratna is a garland of sixty-two -verse hymns submitted to the lotus feet of Lord Vishnu in the spirit of Sharanagati or complete surrender seeking Moksha. These hymns, in delightfully lucid verses, present the central philosophical theme and outlook of VishishtAdvaita doctrine, elucidating its essential principles of Tattva (the intricate relation between God, nature and human); Hita (the excellent path that leads to ones' emancipation); and, Purushartha (the attainment of the supreme goal).

It is said; Sri Vedanta Desika was deeply moved and highly inspired by the <u>28th Sloka of the Stotra-ratna</u>, which extols the virtues of submitting to the Lord, in intense devotion, enormous reverence and deep humility, with folded hands (anjali mudra).

Anjali mudra in front of brahman the supreme god

त्व दङ्घ्रिमुद्दिश्य कदापि केनचिध्यथा
तथावाऽपि सक्त्कृतोऽञ्चलिः |

तदैवमुष्णात्य शुभान्यशेषत
शशऊभआनइपउष्णआतइन जातीहीयते ||२८|

tva daṅghrimuddiśya kadāpi kēnacidhyathā
tathāvā'pi saktkṛtō'ñcaliḥ |
tadaivamuṣṇātya śubhānyaśēṣata –
śśa:ubhaāna:ipa:uṣṇaāta:ina jātīhīyatē ||28||

Oh Lord! When one submits to your sacred feet, with devotion and humility, as Upayam (means) and Phalam (fruit, result) with folded hands (anjali mudra), even once, his past ill-fated Karmas would soon be destroyed ; it would secure freedom from every sort of fear ; and, he would enjoy the blessed joy of residing in your supreme abode of Sri Vaikunta. Such submissions to you with folded hands will surely bring all auspiciousness into one's life.

It is said; when Sri Desika pondered over the essence of this (28th) <u>verse of the Stotra-Ratna</u>, he was struck by the awe-inspiring significance and the immense auspiciousness of this simple gesture of submitting to the Lord with folded hands (*Anjali*) in a spirit of absolute surrender (*Sharanagati, Prapatti*). And, that inspired him to annotate <u>its verse 28 </u> ; to give a detailed exposition of its essence; and, to compose his, now famous, garland of verses under the title <u>*Anjali-vaibhavam*</u> (the glory and splendor of *Anjali*).

Further, it is also said; that Sri Ramanuja was much moved by recitation of the *Stotra-Ratna*; and, that inspired him to compose the <u>*Vaikunta-gadyam*</u>, a pure expression of Bhakti immersed in the spirit of *Atma-nivedana*. - (From -- https://sreenivasaraos.com/tag/siddhi-traya/)

PrajApati and eight Qualities of Atma

Again and again the <u>Upaniṣads</u> glorify Self-knowledge, but what is the nature of the Self, and how do we attain that knowledge? Here the <u>Upaniṣad</u> begins a story to answer this. Once Prajāpati, the creator, decided to teach people about the Self. He described the Self as *apahata-pāpmā*, free from sins, or blemishes (*pāpa*)—that is to say, it is pure. *Vijara*—it never ages, or decays. *Vimṛtyu*—it is free from death.

य आत्मापहतपाप्मा विजरो विमृत्युर्विशोको विजिघत्सोऽपिपासः सत्यकामः सत्यसंकल्पः सोऽन्वेष्टव्यः स विजिज्ञासितव्यः स सर्वांश्च लोकानाप्नोति सर्वांश्च कामान्यस्तमात्मनमनुविद्य विजानातीति ह प्रजापतिरुवाच॥

(छा. उप. ८.७.१)

ya ātmāpahatapāpmā vijarō vimṛtyurviśōkō vijighatsō'pipāsaḥ satyakāmaḥ satyasaṁkalpaḥ sō'nveṣṭavyaḥ sa vijijñāsitavyaḥ sa sarvāṁśca lōkānāpnōti sarvāṁśca kāmānyastamātmanamanuvidya vijānātīti ha prajāpatiruvāca || (chā. upa. 8.7.1)

Word by word meaning

1.Yaḥ <u>ātmā</u> apahatapāpmā- the Self is free from sin;

2.vijaraḥ-free from the effects of age;

3.vimṛtyuḥ-free from death;

4.<u>viśokaḥ</u>- free from sorrow;

5.vijighatsaḥ- free from hunger;

6.apipāsaḥ- free from thirst;

7.<u>satyakāmaḥ</u>- is the cause of desire for Truth;

8.satyasaṅkalpaḥ- is the cause of commitment to Truth;

saḥ, that;

anveṣṭavyaḥ- has to be sought;

saḥ vijijñāsitavyaḥ- that has to be thoroughly investigated;

saḥ- a person;

sarvān ca lokān āpnoti- attains all worlds;

sarvān ca kāmān- and all desires;

yaḥ- who;

tam ātmānam, that Self;

anuvidya-having learned;

 vijānāti- [and] knows it;

prajāpatiḥ iti ha uvāca- Prajāpati said so.

The body, of course, is subject to decay and it perishes. When you look at an old person you can tell at once that the body has decayed. It has become weak, and there are wrinkles and grey hair, and so on. Then gradually it must perish. That which has birth also has death. No matter when the body was born, it will eventually begin to fall apart and die. But the Self will never die. Then Prajāpati says, the Self is _viśoka_, without sorrow, _vijighatsa_, not subject to hunger, and _apipāsa_, not subject to thirst. Besides this, the Self is _satyakāma_ and _satyasaṅkalpa_—seeking the Truth and always rooted in Truth. That is to say, it is Truth- (**ज्ञानम्**) itself. It is always one with Truth, so it can never deviate from Truth.

"Saḥ anveṣṭavyaḥ"—that has to be known. **This is the purpose of life**. Sri Ramakrishna used to say, **'To realize God is the goal of life.'** The goal is not money, not power, not scholarship. It is nothing but God. _Saḥ vijijñāsitavyaḥ_— **it has to be enquired about**. You cannot sit back and wait for it to reveal itself to you. You must go and find someone to teach you about it. And when you have found a capable teacher, you must fall at his feet and beg him to teach you. Then you must ask again and again until your doubts are removed:

'Is it like this? Is it like that?' But you must go to someone who knows the Self. Can a blind man lead another blind man? If the teacher does not know the Self, how will you learn?

When you fulfil these conditions, what happens? You get everything you want. You become supreme. The **Upaniṣad says, you conquer the whole universe**. How? **In this way too, all your desires are fulfilled**. Self-knowledge gives you the step to realize the highest, supreme God,the Brahmam. You may have everything else—friends, relatives, great political power, money, scholarship, a high

social standing—but if you do not have Self-knowledge, Brahmam's knowledge and the relation between these two, everything is useless. Prajāpati has declared: ' 'Come and learn from me.' Here, in order to teach the nature of the Self, and Brahman, and also to emphasize the need for self-discipline to attain Self-knowledge one must find a Guru and take Upadesam from him.

NyAsa VidyA

<u>Brahma SutrA 3.3.56 and 3.3.57 speaks up the following:</u>

Despite different means of UpAsanA in the thirty two VidyAs, there is a freedom of choice in regard to DhyAnA.The out come of results would be same and there is no difference in the same. In order to reach Brahman after realsing the self there are two routes:

1.Bakthi, 2.Prapatti. Both are independent routes to attaining liberation (MokshA-realisation of Brahmam). However, NyAsa is excellent and preffeerred route. AtmA already has the above eight qualities as potential, and are manifested when this Liberation(MokshA) happens. Bakthi YogA is a steep and difficult path since it cannot be practised easily by everyone. Sri.Bagavat RamAnujA in his Gita Bhashyam while expresses the meaning of :

$$\text{सर्वधर्मान्परित्यज्य मामेकं शरणं व्रज ।}$$

$$\text{अहं त्वां सर्वपापेभ्यो मोक्षयिष्यामि मा शुच: || BG. 18.66||}$$

> sarva-dharmān parityajya mām ekaṁ śharaṇaṁ vraja |
>
> ahaṁ tvāṁ sarva-pāpebhyo mokṣhayiṣhyāmi mā śhuchaḥ ||

says,

Since Bagavat Gita is a Bakthi Yoga grantha, this sloka is only to surrender to God and seek, Bakthi YogA ends without any hinderance. However in His SaraNAgati Gatyam He surrenders to Lord RanganathA and ThAyAr, and shows us the path to MokshA is simple, by Prapatti only. Swami Desikan also expresses this is "the Tiruvullam"(This Prapatti is in His mind) of Sri.Bagavat RamAnujA, and advocates Prapatti is preferred to Bakthi.(Kalakshepam of Ahobila Mutt AstAna Vidwan Vaikunta Vasi Sri.Mannarkudi RajagopalAchAriAr) Prapatti is said as "NyAsa VidyA in Brahma UpAsanam.

NyAsa-VidyA requies a deep desire to attain Lord's feet(MokshA) and the firm faith and belief in His protective ability(रक्षगत्वम्) by a JivA. Also other requirements are, to express his utter helplessness to follow any other form of YogA to attain self realisation followed by realisation of Brahmam. There are

74

five AngAs along with one Angi- Surrender (the Sixth) and Swami Desikan in His Rahasya Traya Saram, Chapter -4, Artha PancakA-advocates,that Artha Pancakam or ShadArtham are not different. The Artha PancakAs are five elements a JivA should know by Brahma VidyA through a Guru(AchAryA) and they are:

1. To know about Brahma Swaroopam,

2. To know about Jiva Swaroopm

3. What is UpAyam for Moksha(both UpAyam and UpEyam are Sriman NarAyaNA)

4. Result of this DhyAnam-i.e. Moksham(Realisation of Brahmam)

5. Enemy for MokshA PrApti and Remedy for the same.

6. The sixth one is total Surrender of AtmA itself to Brahmam.

After understanding the Five AngAs actual surrender to Brahmam with the help of a Guru is the Angi.

How NyAsa VidyA is performed:
Essence of NyAsa VidyA is to surrender completely to Brahmamwith the help of a Guru, and enter-into His Kainkaryam (SevA- serve Him in all possible ways). NyAsa vidyA says: NyAsa, the surrender to Brahmam is the highest form of everything one could do. To leave SamsArA, surrender, and submit to Him all our responsibilities and burden (भार) is NyAsa. NyAsa, the surrender to Brahmam is the highest form of everything says this VidyA:

न्यास इत्याहुः मनीषिणो ब्रह्माणं ब्रह्मा विश्वः कतमः स्वयम्भुः प्रजापतिः संवत्थ्सर इति॥

nyāsa ityāhuḥ manīṣiṇō brahmāṇaṁ brahmā viśvaḥ katamaḥ svayambhuḥ prajāpatiḥ saṁvatsara iti. | |

ब्रह्मणे त्वा महस ओमित्यात्मानं युञ्जीतैतद्वै महोपनिषदम्‌|

brahmaṇē tvā mahasa āōmityātmānaṁ yuñjītaitadvai mahōpaniṣadam |

nyAsa VidyA recommends,that in order to liberate and attain MokshA, a jiVa has to understsnd that Brahmam is the means and Brahmam is the Goal also. Then like PraNavA mantrA is used in yAgA for committed devotion of putting DravyA in YagA, one has to give away his own Atma(Prtyag-AtmA) to Him.

Post Prapatti- (NyAsA) how one should conduct is spelt out in detail by Swami Desikan in His, Rahasya traya sAram. One has to consider the entire Life and follow the same as a YogA, and await the day when he will leave

SamsArA and this world to travel to the location where Brahmam is situated,(Vaikuntam) through ArchirAdhi Marga (Path). **From this we know that NyAsa VidyA is an easier alternative to Bakthi YogA.**

14. Bibliography

1. Purusha Suktam from श्वेताश्वतरोपनिषद्- Swetasvatara Upanishad -8-
   https://upanishads.org.in/upanishads/9/3/8

   https://www.google.co.in/search?q=from+where+this+verse+is+taken+

2. Subhashitani Collections from Net.

   N https://www.facebook.com/shdve/posts/1360622764454114

   https://www.tititudorancea.com/z/brahmavidya_upanishad_sanskrit_dev_anagari

3. Selections from Minor Upanishads, translated by K. N. Aiyar, 1914 -
   http://oaks.nvg.org/minor-upanishads.html

4. Brahma Vidya (Chandogya Ch.8) Kindle Edition

5. Ubhaya Vedanta Grantha Mala, Srimad Bhagavad Gita, with Srimad Bhagavad Ramanuja's Bhashya, and Srimad Vedanta Desika's Tatparya Chandrika and Srimad Abhinava Desika Uttamur Viraraghavacharya's detailed Introduction and Rasavada Foot notes. Sri. Uttamur Viraraghavacharya's, centenary Trust, Chennai

6. श्रीव्यासकृत ब्रह्मसूत्राणि, by 44th Pontiff (Azagiya Singer), Sri Ahobila Matam.

7. Nava Ratna Malika, Sri Bhashyam of Sri. Ramanujar with Tamil Transliteration by Sri. U. Ve Tirumalai Caturvedi Shatakrutu Navalpakkam. V. Vasudevachariyar (Vol II, III), Vainavan Kural Publication, Chennai-78, First Publication- Vol II-2017 & VOLIII-2020

8. Wikipedia on "Brahma Vidya"

9. "Yogapedia on "Brahma Vidya"

10. Tamil book written and published by Dr. Venkatesh MBBs., CCEBDM, MBA. He is a ShishyA of Villur NadAdur, Sri Bhashya SimhAsanam, SAstra SAhitee, Vallaba Vidvanmani, Dr. Sri. MatuPayave, KarunAkarArya Maha Desikan. The name of the book is Sri Vidyaigalum and Sri. Rajagopalnum (ஸ்ரீவித்தையைகளும்ஸ்ரீராஜகோபாலனும்.), மன்னார்குடி ஸ்ரீராஜகோபாலன் செய்தருளியலீலைகளும், அவை உணர்த்தும் உபநிஷத் ப்ரஹ்ம வித்தையைகளும். (All LeelAs done by BhagavAn Sri. Mannarkudi Rajagopalan and the way they indicate Upanishad Brahma VidyAs)

11. An introduction to 32 Brahma Vidyas, Secret Doctrines, by Sr. K. R. Krishnaswami., Paduka Krupa, A & K Prakashana, Sep 2011.

12. Srimath Rahasya Traya sAram, Sri Poundarikapuram Swami Asramam, Srirangam published book.-first edition -1960. Proof reading by Sri.U.Ve. VidvAn oppiliappan sannidhi, Vangeepuram Navaneetham Sri.Ramadesikachariar Swami.

13. The Yoga Upanishad's,Sanskrit Text with Commentary of

14. Sri.Upanishad   -Brahmayogin-First edition 2019, Jain Amar printing Press-New delhi   (ISBN: 978-81-8315-354-6)